# CAN YOU RE⌐

## THINK AND GROV

### KEYS TO UNLOCK AN EXTRAORDINARY LIFE

Ramy El-Batrawi

## EXTRAORDINARY LIFE PUBLICATIONS

# FOREWORD

## BY JOHN GRAY

T his short book is a page turner. It is an easy read, and it can change your life. It is a true feel-good, rags-to-riches saga. I couldn't put it down, and I plan to read it again and again.

With complete transparency and vulnerability, the author, Ramy El-Batrawi, not only shares his inspiring journey to enormous riches and great success but outlines the path for everyone to follow.

I have known Ramy for more than 25 years, and I have witnessed his "green thumb" to achieve unimaginable success for himself and for others. I am lucky to have received this support in my own life.

I am the author of the international best seller, *Men Are From Mars, Women Are From Venus* (and many more). Most likely you or your parents have read it or at least have heard of it. With the support of Ramy's genius in marketing and success, we have sold over 50 million books around the world, topping the best-seller lists for over five years and making it the biggest selling relationship book of all time.

When I wrote *Men Are From Mars, Women Are From Venus*, I had hoped to get on the best-seller lists, but with his help, it stayed at the top. Without Ramy's vision and support, it would not have become so widely known and available to the masses.

i

In every chapter of this book, you will discover a secret mindset with specific keys to success that he uses that can awaken within your mind and heart the power to make your dreams come true. I have witnessed Ramy apply each of them, and they work. I use them in my own life.

This secret mindset was first revealed in 1937 by Napoleon Hill in his classic, time-tested, best-selling book, *Think and Grow Rich*. At that time, a small group of individuals who were initiated into this knowledge went on to become the most successful and influential individuals of the last century.

Millions of readers over the last hundred years have greatly benefited from the many insights in *Think and Grow Rich*, but not all. Critics will sometimes complain, "The book only focuses on positive thinking and does not teach you in specific terms what actions to take." In some cases, people just "don't get it." They come away thinking, "If I just imagine success, believe in myself, maintain a positive attitude, and really, really want it, then it will happen. This is certainly a part of the story, but it is clearly not enough."

That is why Ramy's story is the perfect companion to *Think and Grow Rich*. It not only reveals to you the many secrets and keys to success but also inspires and motivates you to take the correct actions. As he recounts how he applied the lessons of *Think and Grow Rich*, he clearly reveals to you what actions you need to take.

Knowledge becomes true power when it is put into action. If you don't apply and test out this secret millionaire mindset with action, then positive thinking alone does little to help you make your dreams come true.

Success comes through increasing your true power. For example, if you want to grow your muscles and become stronger, you have to test them to their limit again and again. You have to feel the burn. Your muscles need to "break down," and then after a few days to recover, when you return to the gym, you will be stronger. Continued growth means many breakdowns.

It is the same with success. The higher your goals, the more breakdowns you must face. One of the many keys to success you will discover is to pick yourself back up and start again. There are no failures in this world, only those who didn't get back up. With the right mindset, every failure contains an insight to help you pivot and achieve even more that you could have imagined.

Understanding the hidden secrets revealed in *Think and Grow Rich* is one thing, but putting them into action is another. With sincere study, in our minds we can easily understand the secrets for success, but it is in our hearts where we find the motivation to take action.

Ramy's journey to success is not just exciting and fascinating—it will land in your heart to activate your inner courage to take action again and again, to pick yourself up when life knocks you down, as he did.

In *Think and Grow Rich*, you hear the stories of successful people. You hear their hardships and challenges but not in their own words. When you read a book about others, your mind will automatically resonate with the ideas and the stories. But the mind does not inspire action. For many, they will think about it but not take action.

As you hear in his own words Ramy's many trials and tribulations as well as his glorious success and fulfillment, these secrets will be implanted in your heart. You too will feel, *If he can do it, then I can do it.*

It is this activation of your heart that can give you the courage and needed motivation to take action and never give up. As you begin to put this secret wisdom of the rich and famous into action, you will know with certainty that you too can think and grow rich.

# ACKNOWLEDGMENTS

I want to thank the Napoleon Hill Foundation for its encouragement, as well as maintaining the powerful legacy of Napoleon Hill's work. If you are committed to achieving great success, please check out what the Foundation has to offer, including correct editions of Hill's books.

I especially want to thank everyone who trusted and invested in me. Though I mention a few by name in this book, there are many others who have joined with me in the same powerful vision of success.

I also am indebted to all my "teachers," whoever or whatever they were, for lessons that propelled me forward in life, including what I learned from loss and temporary pain, never letting negative events overshadow life's great possibilities.

Finally, I want to acknowledge the power of the universe itself, a power that can be tapped by those willing to open their minds to its possibilities.

# Note on Quotations and Keys

This book contains quotations from Napoleon Hill that continue to inspire me, followed by my brief reflections. My adaptations of the principles for unlocking an Extraordinary Life are marked with a key symbol ( 🔑 ).

# Contents

# Introduction:

## Can You Really *Think and Grow Rich?*

My own journey to success began when I first read Napoleon Hill's *Think and Grow Rich* from start to finish.

I was swept up into the book's powerful message, immediately committing to its core principles. At the time, I was 12 years old.

Youth generally makes us more susceptible, more open to new ideas. As we grow older, outside influences begin to form and mold our minds into something potentially rigid and inflexible. In the case of *Think and Grow Rich*, I was young and open enough, fortunately, to let Hill's words take up residence in my mind, one of the many opportunities that I would pursue with complete commitment throughout my life.

I say *opportunities* and not *luck* since what I have accomplished—and continue to accomplish—is not a matter of luck but instead a demonstration that, if we fully commit to the central principles of *Think and Grow Rich*, we can be wildly successfully, learning how to master destiny no matter what is thrown into our paths. Even the worst-seeming events and their attendant suffering are yet further opportunities for making us stronger and thus more successful. I learned at the very beginning of my journey how to move fluidly and decisively as opportunities arose, all in the spirit of Napoleon Hill. As you read this book, think about how you can do the same today, tomorrow, and on into the future.

Since its publication in 1937, *Think and Grow Rich* has created more millionaires than any other book ever written, providing a roadmap to whatever success readers desire, though, as I discuss later, that must be a fully-committed, burning desire, a "Master Key," according to Hill. His book jumpstarted the self-help industry—its influence can be traced through Tony Robbins, Jack Canfield, Eckhart Tolle, and many, many others—and remains a bestseller to this day.

———————○———————

There is a difference between WISH-ING for a thing and being READY to receive it. No one is ready for a thing, until he believes he can acquire it. The state of mind must be BELIEF, not mere hope or wish. Open-mindedness is essential for belief.

— *Think and Grow Rich*

———————○———————

I've met many people who insist that they are "open-minded" yet clearly have mental barriers that block progress toward their goals. The "belief" that *Think and Grow Rich* discusses should always result in clear, decisive action.

I decided to write this book for two reasons. First, I wanted to show you, the reader, how I systematically tested and applied Hill's principles throughout my life in order to learn how to achieve success. Second, I wanted to use my own experiences to help you translate the principles of *Think and Grow Rich* into action so that you too can achieve the success that otherwise often eludes people who turn to self-help books.

My experience clearly answers the question posed by this book's title: Yes, you *can* think and grow rich. We can personalize this further: Yes, *you*—not someone else, but you, the reader of this book—can think and grow rich. If you don't believe in yourself, why would anyone else do so?

In addition to demonstrating how the main principles of *Think and Grow Rich* have worked in my life, I also will describe how I extended and refined the principles for my own use. Hill's life work was devoted to teaching others how to make his principles their own. Every step of the way, I ingrained Hill's principles into my everyday thinking so that they became my natural way of facing the world.

I don't stop to consider how I should react to a new situation but instead automatically and confidently move forward. My default switch is always *on*, always channeling what I take away from *Think and Grow Rich* as well as the inspirational stories of others who can help fortify our aspirations. Upscale hotels often have upper floors that can only be accessed with special key cards—I want to inspire others not only to leave the lobby but also use their own keys to rise past the lower floors into the stratospheric levels of life.

My continuing journey to success, as you will see, wasn't the clichéd story that supposedly moves steadily from an ordinary life to a successful one:

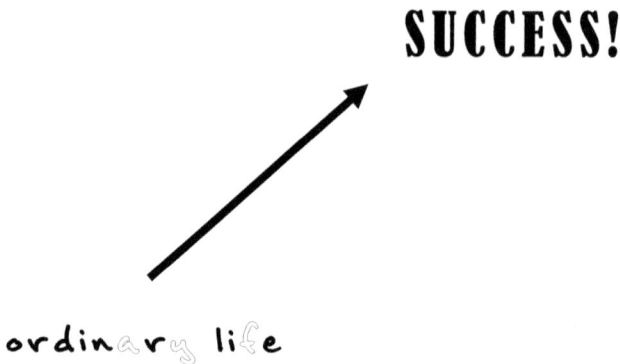

**SUCCESS!**

ordinary life

Instead, it was set of seismic events that likely would have destroyed many—perhaps most—others' ability to function.

Not only did I succeed in reaching each goal I set for myself, I learned that I could break out of limitations that others tried to impose on me as well as on themselves. Instead of letting anyone or anything draw a boundary around my ambition, I decided to keep striving for an *Extraordinary Life*:

We can live extraordinary lives by infusing our waking hours with clear inspiration that frees us from doubt and fear, as well as other habits that hold us back and block our progress.

I happened to be ready to receive the message of *Think and Grow Rich* when I was 12, but whatever your age, you must, as Hill insists, fully believe, fully commit to the path that I and others who strive for success continue to walk every day if you too wish to live an extraordinary life. You must fully accept that you can indeed *think and grow rich*.

Reaching the top level of any field is difficult, time-consuming, and often tedious. The reason that you can fail to reach this level of success—and most people do fail—is that *saying* you are fully committed is easy. But it's the action that counts, just like placing your bet and pushing in all of your poker chips: You must develop a reputation for being willing to go all in when necessary.

Those who don't fully commit are likely to give up when the going gets tough. There's no doubt, as my own life demonstrates, that there will be tough times. One step you can take today to fortify yourself is to seek inspiration in the biographies of men and women who have achieved greatness in their lives. You will find that they prevailed because they refused to quit, pushing on long after the masses had given up and gone home. These men and women become your peers—you should believe that you belong in their circle. If you do not, then how can you ever walk the path to success?

This book recounts what I think of as my own extraordinary life, which included building wealth. But the takeaway is not just this or that particular accomplishment but how, no matter how many times

I have fallen, I stood right back up, as I would do again if necessary. I believe that this trait is my bedrock strength, just as it has been for other successful people I admire.

I conduct my business and personal life with transparency and sincerity and will give you unvarnished details of my life so that you can learn from them. Adapt what I have to offer so that you can build your own extraordinary life—starting *today*.

You know, there's a philosopher who says, "As you live your life, it appears to be anarchy and chaos, and random events, non-related events, smashing into each other and causing this situation or that situation, and then, this happens, and it's overwhelming, and it just looks like what in the world is going on? And later, when you look back at it, it looks like a finely crafted novel. But at the time, it don't."

—Joe Walsh

By keeping the principles of *Think and Grow Rich* present in my mind, I never let the chaos of life defeat me. Instead, I learned to plan and order every single day.

# CHAPTER 1:

## NO EXCUSES, NO ALIBIS

T he final chapter of *Think and Grow Rich* identifies the common excuses for not succeeding in life—or for failing to even start on the road to success.

Just as I decided to reject all of them, you should examine these, as well as potentially countless others, in order to determine whether you are using alibis as excuses, then do the essential work of casting them aside.

Here are some of the *Ifs* identified in *Think and Grow Rich* that are used as *alibis* (they are lightly edited):

*If* I didn't have a spouse and family.

*If* I only had somebody to help me.

*If* I had enough "pull."

*If* I had money.

*If* I had a good education.

*If* I could get a job.

*If* I had good health.

*If* I only had time.

*If* times where better.

*If* people understood me.

*If* conditions where only different.

*If* I could live my life over.

*If* I did not fear what they would say.

*If* had been given a chance.

*If* people did not have it in for me.

*If* I were only younger.

*If* I only embraced past opportunities.

*If* my family understood me.

*If* I lived in a big city.

*If* I could just get started.

*If* I were only free.

*If* I could just get a break.

*If* I could only get out of debt.

*If* I hadn't failed.

*If* I only knew how.

*If* everybody didn't oppose me.

*If* I were sure of myself.

*If* luck were not against me.

*If* I had not been born under the wrong star.

*If* I had not lost all my money.

*If* I only could do what I want.

*If* I had a different past.

*If* I had been born rich.

*If* I only had a business of my own.

*If* I could meet the right people.

*If* other people would listen to me.

*If* I had the talent that some people have.

*If* I had courage to see myself as I really am.

*If* I could save money.

Have you ever used one of these or a similar excuse? Many people lean on such alibis not only to justify a lack of success, but also why they never even attempted to achieve their dreams. I certainly could have defaulted to any of these alibis and many more. After all, I dropped out of school at 12, left home, and remained homeless until I was 17. Yet I learned to reject all of the *Ifs*, as should you.

### *Ignore Luck.*

I avoid using the word *luck*, especially when people tell me that they just wished that they had better luck or could catch a lucky break. They may believe that success, especially financial riches, come to the lucky, and they look for some way to become that lucky gambler. But if you think this way, just as the "house" always wins in the long run in a casino, so will life beat you down. As I demonstrate on my own journey to success, I never expected lucky breaks, though I did pivot instantly to take advantage of clear opportunities.

*Ignore Fear.*

In addition to the *Ifs*, the last chapter of *Think and Grow Rich* also covers the six basic "ghosts" or fears that often hang over people, preventing them from achieving success: the fear of poverty, the fear of criticism, the fear of illness, the fear of losing love, the fear of old age, and the fear of death. But I overcame the fears, as well as what Hill calls the seventh basic evil: susceptibility to negative influences.

I began with nothing, gained great wealth many times, lost that wealth, and then rebuilt and surpassed my previous accomplishments. I ultimately triumphed over the constant negative influences that surrounded me in the world, particularly those naysayers who insisted that I would never achieve what seemed to them an impossible goal.

*Positive Thinking Is Not Enough.*

Before I embarked on my journey to success and an extraordinary life, I had no education, no money, and no friends—no thought I would succeed at anything. The fear of poverty could have easily crippled me, but understanding the principles of *Think and Grow Rich* helped me to overcome obstacles that otherwise could have blocked me from achieving my goals. In fact, I stopped thinking about *obstacles* and instead always translated them into *opportunities* that I could exploit by shifting immediately as needed.

I learned how to shift in whatever direction was optimal, except for one: I never moved backwards, never looked over my shoulder to the past with regret. I made the ability to shift or pivot my default way of acting, one I maintain to this day.

*Think and Grow Rich* is not only about positive thinking: Just having a thin layer of positive thinking over an ocean of negative thoughts will not generate a successful life, let alone an extraordinary one. Eventually all the negative thoughts, all your fears, will flood the layer of positive thinking, which is why you must understand that just reading an inspirational book will not propel you forward. Instead, any useful principles must be ingrained in both your conscious mind and your subconscious mind: The principles should dominate your thoughts completely so that there is no room for negativity to seep back in. This is a point that I will come back to repeatedly.

The journey of a thousand miles begins with a single step." You have
probably known people nearing the
end of their life's journey who looked
back and said, "If only I had done
things differently.... If only I had
taken advantage of that opportunity
when it came along." Unfulfilled lives
are filled with "if onlys." They are the
refrain of the timid souls whose lives
were finished before they ever really
got started. Life is filled with many
opportunities—for great successes and
spectacular failures. It is up to you to
seize the initiative, to take advantage
of the opportunities that come your
way. You are condemned to a life of
mediocrity—unless you get into action. Don't delay; do it today!

—*Think and Grow Rich*

I aim for the highest level and never
settle, no matter the risk, for a life of
mediocrity.

## The Master Key of Think and Grow Rich.

Just *thinking* about something is not enough. You must build an intense, burning desire. Without that burning desire, at the first sign of adversity, you probably will quit.

That burning desire is what keeps you going no matter how many roadblocks you face, no matter how many times you hear the word *No*, and no matter how many times you are rejected. On the very last page of *Think and Grow Rich*, Hill emphasizes that a burning desire is the "Master Key" that unlocks wealth.

The burning desire was the first key. From there, I assembled other keys that unlock the doors leading to an Extraordinary Life.

## The First Key That Opens Doors.

Everyone wants something, whether it's great wealth, great love, or great influence. But a powerful desire, especially a true burning desire, is far more than this and is acquired through a basic principle advocated in *Think and Grow Rich*, one which I employ every day:

*Mix what you want with intense emotions in order to drive you to ever greater success.*

The emotions you mix with your thoughts do not necessarily have to be positive. Emotions of great love and great sex, for example, are powerful, but emotions such as intense pain are potentially just as effective. Even the emotions created by certain chemicals can be powerful—that's why some of the greatest music has been created by musicians who have experimented with psychedelic drugs.

In my own case, I applied two of *Think and Grow Rich*'s main principles at the beginning of my journey:

*Whatever your mind can conceive and believe, you can achieve.*

*By mixing intense emotion with what you want to achieve, you can achieve anything.*

Constantly believing in, as well as applying, these principles will help you achieve the focus needed for reaching your goals. And the more focused you become, the more that these principles will infuse your daily life.

You must be relentless in order to succeed.

*Determination and a burning desire can never be stopped.*

### Burning Desire and the Coral Castle.

After leaving home when I was 12, I had no particular destination in mind other than the US. I happened to end up in Florida, where, as I started my journey to success, I paid close attention to other people's experiences, constantly relating *Think and Grow Rich*'s teachings to what others had achieved.

One of my first discoveries was the Coral Castle, a tourist attraction first built in Florida City and then moved by its owner to what is now Homestead, near Miami. The home and its surrounding grounds are an extraordinary testament to what the human mind can conceive and then achieve. Ed Leedskalnin spent 28 years carving—using only handmade tools—over a thousand tons of Oolite (a sedimentary rock that often includes fossil shells and actual coral) into monumental structures such as a tower where he lived, furniture, and sculptures. Every block is arranged without mortar and with such precision that a thin knife cannot be inserted between the joints. A gate, one of the most famous attractions and weighing over eight tons, is so finely balanced that it can be opened with the shove from a single finger.

The standard story is that Leedskalnin, then 26 and still in his homeland of Latvia, was jilted by his fiancé the day before their impending wedding. After he immigrated to the United States, Leedskalnin harnessed the intense negative emotion from the rejection in order to create a burning desire. Though he was around 100 pounds and just over 5 feet tall, by opening his mind to the universe, he learned the secrets of how to build, by himself, an astounding monument to his true love.

The Coral Castle demonstrated clearly to me that, if you mix powerful emotions with what you desire, nothing can stop you from achieving your goals, just as nothing stopped Leedskalnin. The Castle became a sort of blueprint for building my own burning desire.

Leedskalnin never gave up the secrets of how exactly he built the Coral Castle. I, however, am not holding back any secrets for success. I'm going to show you both highs and lows, all of which turned out to be essential to my eventual greater success.

*Part of the Coral Castle.*

*Empty Pockets, Rich Mind.*

When I left home, I owned virtually nothing except *Think and Grow Rich*, which I had already read over 20 times. I was surprised that I intuitively and immediately grasped many of its principles. Later in life, I realized all this knowledge is really already out there in the universe. *Think and Grow Rich* just opened my eyes to what I really already knew on some deeper level. I was ready to receive the basic truths of Hill's work, and when something is based in truth, it will stand the test of time.

My next task was to constantly maintain the burning desire to succeed. Without such desire, I could not have survived on the streets for five years, which is where I lived after landing in Florida. Many people would have just returned home while thinking, *This is just too damn hard.* Many people would have given up on the dream of becoming wealthy and successful.

Before you can build anything worthwhile, you must first create it in your mind. Your mind is not constrained by physical limitations or boundaries. In the workshop of your mind, you can visualize things that have never been. It is said that Albert Einstein visualized how the universe might look if he were riding astride a beam of light through infinity. Then he worked out the mathematics to support his theory of relativity. You can use the power of your imagination to visualize solutions to difficult problems, to develop new ideas, and to see yourself achieving the goals you have set for yourself.

*—Think and Grow Rich*

I constantly use my mind's "workshop" to generate creative ideas for new projects. The workshop is open and active 24/7.

The burning desire I built in myself kept me going every single day until I figured out what it took to start achieving success.

# CHAPTER 2:

## ON THE STREETS OF LIFE

My philosophy is to look forward rather than regret the past. We've all heard hard-luck stories that are convenient alibis, but though I started my journey literally homeless and on the streets of Tampa, Florida, I consider that time my first testing ground for the ideas in *Think and Grow Rich*.

### First Choices.

I was born in Geneva, Switzerland, to Egyptian parents. We moved from Geneva to Paris, then to the US for two years, then on to Montreal, Quebec. I wasn't academically motivated, often failing my classes (the last years of my formal education were more like those in a US high school), but I did learn about the hard knocks of life. I was the kid picked out for bullying, an experience that I used later not only to toughen myself, but also decide that if one day I had power over others, I would not use that position to bully and intimidate. Instead, I would treat everyone the same regardless of their wealth or status.

Those years also instilled a powerful motivation to achieve as much as possible in my life. I didn't begin with much at all, unlike people who are given instant advantages that can sap their ability to handle life's challenges.

My father at one point left the family for six months (he already had divorced my mother, who then went back to Egypt), but his return did not change my mind about my path: I made the choice to leave on my own power since I knew that just sitting at home wouldn't jumpstart my future. In 1973, I set out for the US, a country that offered real opportunities, though I had no idea where I would end up exactly.

I eventually found myself in Tampa, Florida, which at least had the advantage of warm winters, unlike Montreal. I was confident, after reading *Think and Grow Rich*, that I could manage somehow to live on my own.

When I finally arrived in the city, I just started walking and observing, already forming the habit of talking to anyone I met, though I wasn't yet focused on my journey to success. In those days, Tampa was hardly a cosmopolitan city, and was a particularly harsh place for the homeless. Drug dealers, pimps, and the obviously mentally ill crisscrossed the streets and intersections. At first, I slept under one of the highway overpasses.

Fortunately, I looked older than my chronological age, even passing for an adult. I learned to wash up whenever I could in gas station bathrooms. For the next couple of years, I took brief jobs, including helping out in motels and selling products door-to-door. When I learned of a used 1968 Cadillac that was for sale, I worked for three weeks as a short order cook until I had the $300 purchase price.

The unairconditioned car became my home, a relatively secure space in which I could think and plan. The summers were brutal, especially since, in order to escape the clouds of mosquitos at night, I kept the windows rolled up, which meant that the internal temperature could reach 120 degrees before I woke.

Over a couple of years, I developed one clear, overarching goal: *Build great wealth.* I knew that I could not accomplish this goal by working for someone else, so I decided that being my own boss was absolutely essential. As *Think and Grow Rich* points out, if we start out with just modest goals and then stay within a comfortable niche, we are unlikely to develop a truly powerful vision, let alone rise to the highest levels in life.

I had to build businesses of my own if I ever wanted to achieve extraordinary success. No matter how long or difficult the task, I was going to find my first business that would jumpstart my future empire.

### Continuing Inspiration.

As I said, I could dwell on the hardships of my first years in Tampa, but that's not the habit of someone seeking an extraordinary life, and it shouldn't be yours if you also want to step onto a similar path. I looked for inspiration that always faced forward to the future, whether in a book or a person.

That's not to say that I ever forgot or neglected those who helped me when I had nothing. Earl Farris, for example, believed in me after my brief time with Glen Turner's organization, mentioned in the next section. He was willing to mortgage his house for investment funds, and took me to a Piccadilly restaurant every day so that I could eat. He ultimately was not financially successful, but I made sure later to take care of him until the day he died.

*Discard doubt, but do not discard those who have helped you and believed in you.*

I often mention people who have inspired me, no matter whether they provide positive or negative examples—if there is powerful influence involved, there is a strategy worth learning. I also find inspiration in powerful words, such as the following poem I first encountered in *Think and Grow Rich* and have had to reread many times in order to gain its full insight. The poem is by Jessie B. Rittenhouse and expresses what Hill called "the universal truth":

*I bargained with Life for a penny,*

*And Life would pay no more,*

*However I begged at evening*

*When I counted my scanty store.*

*For Life is a just employer,*

*He gives you what you ask,*

*But once you have set the wages,*

*Why, you must bear the task.*

*I worked for a menial's hire,*

*Only to learn, dismayed,*

*That any wage I had asked of Life,*

*Life would have willingly paid.*

Too many times, we set our "wages" too low, keeping our vision too narrow and constrained. Starting today, recalibrate what you ask of Life. Refuse, just as I did, any limits on what you can achieve.

*When you find words that inspire you to a greater future, keep them in the front of your mind at all times.*

*Rejecting the Fear of Loss.*

When I started, I had no money or prospects, but I did believe in myself, that I could achieve anything I set my mind to. I was open to whatever principles or thoughts that would further my goal.

During my time on the streets of Tampa, I learned an essential lesson:

*For most people, the fear of loss is greater than the hope of gain.*

I saw this fear play out again and again, and the concept was crystalized for me when I was invited—I was just 15 years old—to a seminar by Glen Turner, who was a powerful motivational speaker. He ultimately served 6 years in prison on charges of running a pyramid scheme, but whatever his actual intentions, I could tell that he understood how to influence thousands of people at a time, at one point amassing a fortune of over $200 million.

His presentation included a chart that illustrated the basic truth that fear stops most people from achieving great success. Most people start on the same path, perhaps getting their first car by 18 and their first apartment by 21, and then getting married by 23. Then comes a house, a second car, children, and the children's education. They work 9 to 5, go home, watch TV, eat dinner, go to bed, and repeat everything the next day. They live for the weekends and their once-per-year vacations. They live the same routines until they eventually retire with little savings—and then they die.

Turner had purposely painted a bleak picture, but I grasped that here was a fundamental truth about the common fear of loss. Most people will not consider giving up their jobs—even in the service of a greater success—because they fear losing their income and not being able to pay the mortgage or support their family. They remain stuck in a cycle, never challenging life itself for fear of losing the little they have.

The seminar gave me more than insight into the fear of loss. I stood up and gave my own speech—the first time I had given a public one—that so inspired the attendees that several flocked around me, trying to become part of whatever team or company I might form. That in turn got me thrown out of the seminar and back onto the street, but my takeaway was to continue to make my hope of gain greater than my fear of loss.

One of my strengths clearly was the ability to motivate and even inspire others, which I had now demonstrated concretely. This ability would prove to be more valuable than becoming part of anyone's organization, no matter the starting wage. My eventual gain would be achieved using the skills I was practicing on the streets of Tampa.

*Make your hope of gain greater than your fear of loss.*

### Keys to My First Million.

Since the start of my journey at 12, I tried many businesses that mostly failed, but I kept on learning and striving. Again and again, I would brainstorm a moneymaking idea and immediately set to work, and if it fizzled, then I would start again. One day around Christmastime when I was 17 and happened to be standing in front of a Zayre, at the time part of a chain of 400 discount department stores, I recognized the opportunity that would make my first million.

Just outside the main entrance, a man was selling glass swans. As was my default behavior (and still is), I walked up and just started a conversation about his business. I learned that he had rented a front corner for the season, taking advantage of the foot traffic, which resulted in strong sales of his glass swans. It hit me that, if I could find something that I could sell all through the year and not just seasonally, I could create a successful business.

Over the next couple of days, I talked to as many store employees as I could to find out what customers asked for that Zayre didn't carry. I learned that some customers wanted keys duplicated, a service that the store did not provide, and I immediately recognized a need that my new business could meet.

*Find the need and fill it.*

Along the journey to build a successful business, I started to understand that one must always find legitimate needs and then fill them. The only way I could pinpoint such needs was to talk with everyone I could, paying attention to what was missing, what was needed, and what was in demand.

I had no money, I knew nothing about cutting keys, and I had no real access to store management to be able to secure the prime location in front of the store, but I did not let any of that deter me from the goal of starting my first key center.

I managed to scrape together $50 to purchase a used key-making machine. I found an old desk in a junkyard and a cash register lying discarded on a restaurant floor. After being referred to someone who sold key blanks, I promised to buy blanks exclusively from him if he showed me everything there was to know about cutting keys, which he agreed to do.

I sold him a *vision*: I would open many key centers in the future, and his business would expand as mine did.

In my later business deals, I would prosper by drawing on this same ability to build a relatable, believable vision. Everyone whom you bring in needs to become part of this vision, not just passive contributors. It's easy to say, "I'll never forget you," but in my business life, I've made sure to build a reputation for remembering those who maintained their belief in me. Those who join in my vision—no matter what their actual jobs or positions in life—are never just means to an end.

*To achieve an extraordinary life, step with, and not on or over, people who believe in you.*

I approached the store manager, who at first refused to consider any offer, but after I persisted, he agreed for 20% of my gross sales. In the first week alone, I made over $600. I quickly hired someone to staff my kiosk, and over the next year, I opened hundreds of key centers throughout the Zayre chain.

*I found the need and filled it.* I had a definite plan backed by a burning desire, which gave me the persistence I needed to build a net worth of over a million dollars when I was just 17 years old.

Those who will not take a chance seldom have one thrust upon them. Success always involves risk. You must take a chance by investing your time, money, and effort. It pays to be thoughtful and deliberate in your analyses of opportunities, but don't let timidity hold you back. Because you have worked hard to develop those things you must risk, it is natural for you to place a high value on them. But what good are they if you do not put them to use? You will recognize opportunity only to the extent that you are willing to consider risking your time, money, and effort. Being confident gives you the courage to face risk and act when opportunity arises. No one on earth is going to force success upon you; you will find it only to the degree that you actively seek it out.

—*Think and Grow Rich*

I didn't wait for the "perfect" opportunity but instead put my maximum
effort into anything I started.

## More Attention Needed.

Unfortunately, I was still a newbie and needed to learn much more about the nuts and bolts of running a day-to-day business. I didn't pay attention to all of the details, including something as fundamental as having a long-term lease.

The management at Zayre saw how much money was being made from just the 20%. They gave me a 30-day notice to vacate all the stores. Before I knew it, I was broke again, and because I had reinvested all the money in growing my business, I was left penniless and homeless once more, back to sleeping in a car.

Giving up did not occur to me because I still had the burning desire to acquire great wealth. Building the key centers was just one way. There were others—I just had to come up with a new idea.

Failure is a blessing when it pushes us out of a cushioned seat of self-satisfaction and forces us to do some-thing useful. If you carefully study your own life and those of achievers whom you admire, it is an absolute certainty you will discover that your greatest opportunities often occurred during times of adversity. It is only when faced with the possibility of failure that we are willing to deal with radical change and take the risks that lead to great success. When you experience temporary failure and you know that it is temporary, you can capitalize on the opportunities adversity always brings.

—*Think and Grow Rich*

I see even the most dramatic failures as temporary. I never give in to any fears.

# CHAPTER 3:

## BROKE BUT NOT BROKEN

I came to understand that if I wanted to build bigger and faster, I would need to use other people's money, especially if I didn't have any of my own.

This basic tenet of business helped me to achieve so much more success than I otherwise would have in the following years.

*To build bigger and faster, use other people's money.*

This is not a cynical strategy if you keep in mind, as I have, the trust that has been placed in you. No matter what happens in a business deal, I have made it a rule to ensure that investors are paid first, even if that means that I personally take a hit. Many books advise, when setting up a small business, to ensure that you, the owner, are paid first. But if you are going to build extraordinary wealth, which will require leveraging other people's money and potentially their reputations, then consider your priorities carefully.

*When using other people's money, you have to take responsibility, and you have to put them ahead of you.*

### Securing an Investor.

Broke again, I immediately searched for my next business (this was a habit that would become so ingrained that I stay attuned to opportunities even while managing the daily challenges of my current projects). One day, as I once again walked the streets of Tampa, I stopped at a body shop and spoke to the owner who was just inside the open garage. During our conversation, a customer—who had a few cars in the garage, which particularly caught my attention— walked in. Turning to the customer, I learned that he bought cars from auctions, paid to have them repaired, then resold them at another auction. I thought, *This is something I easily could pull off.*

All I needed was someone to put up the money to purchase the car, a strategy I had acquired after my key-making venture. And the Zayre experience offered opportunities, too: I had connected with a police officer who worked security for the store as his third job, which he needed in order to fully support his family. I left the body shop, approached the officer again, and proposed that, if he put up money to purchase the cars, I would buy, repair, and sell them at an auction, after which we would split the profits 50-50. In the meantime, he would hold the car titles as collateral. (The 50-50 split became my default deal.)

> *At all times, have faith in yourself and what you can accomplish.*

Though the first few cars were profitable, I recognized that the profits weren't great enough to help me reach my financial goal. I became much more aggressive, buying cars at a furious pace. In an illustration of the importance of paying attention (or in this case, not paying enough attention), I failed to realize that a Florida title meant that a car under these conditions was considered totaled and thus worth considerably less than I had calculated. I had overspent on the cars and now faced losing my new business venture.

The experience crystalized the principle from *Think and Grow Rich* that adversity, failure, and heartache carry the seeds of equivalent or even greater benefits. I just didn't give up. I was now 21 years old.

When you are determined that you will not allow others to determine your future for you, when you refuse to allow temporary setbacks to defeat you, you are destined for great success. The opportunities will always be there for you. If there are adversities that you cannot overcome right now, remember to capitalize upon them at a later date by looking for the seed of an equivalent or greater benefit.

—*Think and Grow Rich*

— REFLECTION —

By learning the answer to the question, "Who could benefit from this?" I can turn a *no* into a *yes*, and thus the deal becomes a win-win.

## Shifting Gears.

I was down to my last vehicle, a truck that I had repaired and taken to an auction, but it hadn't sold. After the bidding ended, I noticed a man looking over the truck, so I approached him and offered to sell it. He wasn't interested in buying, but after a prolonged conversation, he mentioned an interest in van "shells." Because of new government rules for increased vehicle gas mileage, manufacturers were producing smaller cars and fewer trucks, thus creating a greater demand for vans. Ate the same time, custom vans were becoming all the rage, putting even more pressure on the market.

Van shells presented a new opportunity: a need to be filled.

*Always be ready to shift when you're headed in the wrong direction.*

Be willing to shift does not mean that you should abandon your goals, but instead you must flexible and adjust your strategy for how to achieve those goals. I started out with the concept of buying, fixing, and selling cars, but quickly decided to shift to the custom van business.

Because vans were in short supply, my new business connection promised to pay me for each van shell I found, which he would then build out for resale. With total confidence that I practiced every day on the streets, as well in that first public speech at a Glen Turner meeting, I told him that I would find all the shells he needed.

*Always show confidence when you speak. Others are drawn to those who speak and act confidently.*

## A Brief on Confidence.

I have been asked repeatedly how to gain confidence, but that question reverses the process: Even if initially you lack confidence, move ahead as if you are completely confident. If you present proposals with confidence, people will believe you and trust you. Basically, *fake it till you make it,* which, though a cliché, is based in truth.

I have approached everything in life with total confidence even if I didn't know how I was going to accomplish a task at that moment. I knew I would figure it out. People like dealing with people who are confident rather than arrogant—they will give you the benefit of the doubt.

## Faith and Opportunity.

I had no clue where I could find vans, especially since they were in such short supply. To make matters worse, I did not have the up-front money to purchase the vans in order to resell them as promised. But with a faith in myself that I could accomplish anything, I went out searching and called dealership after dealership until I finally found one in the Florida Panhandle that had 12 vans. I promised the salesman that I would arrive soon to purchase all of them (the Panhandle is at least 6-7 hours away from Tampa by car).

I made the call on a Saturday. The auction, where I had agreed to meet for the purchaser, would be held on Tuesday. I had to figure out how I was to come up with the $150,000 to buy vans while at the same time taking the risk that a relative stranger actually would buy them from me.

I knew that if I approached the salesman with the confidence that I had the money, he would believe me. And it worked: When I arrived, he was excited enough about the sale to accept a $150,000 check.

I knew that the check would hit the bank by Tuesday. If the purchaser did not keep his word, then I would probably go to jail for trying to pass a bad check.

*Success requires taking risks when you have to.*

Once the salesmen accepted the check, I went to a few 7-Elevens, found 12 somewhat tattered-looking guys just hanging around the storefronts, and offered them each $10 to drive the vans back to Tampa, which still was my home base. On Monday morning, I called the bank and asked the bank manager what was the latest he could hold the check before he had to return it on Tuesday, and he gave me a 2:00 pm deadline. On Tuesday morning, I enlisted another 12 men to drive as fast as they could to the auction in Orlando.

The purchaser, fortunately, kept his word and handed me a check for the vans and an additional $600 per van as my profit. At that moment, I realized I had no transportation back to Tampa for the

12 men, let alone for me. Then I confidently told the purchaser that I would sell his custom van back in Tampa, and he handed over the keys.

I loaded up the 12 men and drove as fast as I could to the bank, arriving at 5 minutes before the deadline. To my dismay, the bank manager explained that he could not cover check with another check, and he would have to return the one I had written.

Again, with confidence and persistence, I engaged the bank manager in an hour-long conversation that began face to face and standing and then continued after we sat down together. It was a tough sell, he finally agreed to cover the check.

Overcaution is as bad as no caution. If you expect others to have confidence in you, you must conduct yourself in a way that inspires trust. Being so cautious that you never try anything new will damage your credibility just as much as will throwing all caution to the winds and trying any idea that comes along without thinking it through. (Most people equate any kind of extreme behavior with poor judgment.) But don't fall victim to "analysis paralysis." Learn to separate facts from opinions and make sure your decisions—and your subsequent actions—are based on reliable information. Then take action!"

—*Think and Grow Rich*

I seek out the most reliable information, including a reliable network of people who keep me informed on issues that affect any of my goals.

According to *Think and Grow Rich*, every little success will build your confidence so that you believe in your capabilities more and more. Every success I had in convincing people to perform the tasks I required to further my goals instilled *even more confidence* in my ability to achieve those very goals.

After leaving the bank, I drove the custom van to the first dealership I found, which happened to be next door. While I was selling the manager on buying the van, a customer was simultaneously keenly interested, walking around and peering into the vehicle.

The manager, who also noticed the customer's interest, cut short our conversation and bought the van from me, generating another $600 profit. I stayed behind to watch the dealership sell the van at a $6,000 profit. I realized then that the real money was in selling the vans retail.

*A 1980s custom Ford van.*

## Who Will Benefit?

I learned that, when you want to achieve something, have someone invest in you, or have a customer or vendor support you, always think of who will benefit by your winning. When you present an idea, you are not selling something you want—you are selling what someone else will gain, which makes his or her decision much easier. Chances are that the answer will be a *Yes*.

I also learned that, when you structure a deal, you have to make sure everyone wins. If even one person loses in any negotiation or deal, the deal is a bad one and usually will not work out.

*A good deal = everyone wins.*

Over the next four months, I bought van shells and then sold them to the custom van manufacturer, after which I would sell custom vans to dealerships, all the while wracking my brain, trying to think of who would benefit from my owning a dealership. It hit me that the manufacturer of vans would benefit more by selling their vans through their own dealerships rather than selling the vans here and there through auctions and other dealerships.

I decided that I would approach a van manufacturer and propose that, if the company would put up approximately $1 million to open up a dealership and provide all the vans I needed to sell, the company's profits would increase enormously. I structured what became my standard deal that used the split I mentioned earlier: Someone puts up the money, I do all the work, and we split the profits 50-50.

I drove to Hartwell. Georgia, where the manufacturing facility was located. It was no easy task, but I finally convinced the owner to put up $1 million and 100 vans to open up my first dealership. I didn't just create a single profitable business but instead pushed forward to ever greater success. In just two years, I built six dealerships, started an insurance company, and invested in real estate. By the age of 23, I had built a net worth of over $50 million.

The most important job is that of learning how to negotiate with others. Experts in negotiation handle the process so smoothly that discussions hardly seem like negotiations at all. While the word negotiation itself conjures up visions of cigar-chomping adversaries pounding the table to emphasize their demands, the best results are achieved when all the parties involved are able to put themselves in the others' shoes and arrive at an agreement that is beneficial to everyone involved…. [Y]our chances of success are far greater when you approach the situation positively and with a clear objective in mind. It also helps to understand the motives of others involved and to have in-depth knowledge of the subject under discussion. Finally, approach every topic with an open mind—don't simply try to bully others into accepting your proposal or point of view.

—*Think and Grow Rich*

I let others speak, rather than just jumping in to overwhelm them with my ideas. I manage positive negotiations using a tactic that others often lack: patience.

# CHAPTER 4:

## LOSS AND GAIN WITH KHASHOGGI

I was 24, a multimillionaire, and one of the richest men in Tampa.

I was sure that I had secured everything that counted as success: For example, I purchased an estate, which I proceeded to fill with aviaries and other markers of sophistication, that was a former botanical garden along the Hillsborough River. I drove a De Tomaso, one of the rarest sportscars at the time. I had spent over a decade in Florida, with many more adventures than I have described, but finally, I thought, I had reached my goal of achieving great wealth and success.

### Shifting My Vision, Throwing Off Complacency.

I invited some acquaintances over for a TV night premier of a one-hour special edition of *Lifestyles of the Rich and Famous.*

The show focused on Adnan Khashoggi, then considered the richest man in the world, and showcased his homes (he owned 35), jets, helicopters, yacht, and the overall gilded lifestyle he had built, described in the program as the "ultimate lifestyle that money could buy." But what really captured my imagination was host Robin Leach's description of Khashoggi as *a head of state without a state*, someone who not only structured billion-dollar transactions but also commanded respect from political leaders throughout the world.

*Adnan Khashoggi.*

True, the images of the tangible physical objects were striking, but my focus was on the scenes of his sitting side by side with world leaders, literally on their same level. Khashoggi's influence, his power, and his life represented what could become my own trajectory that began when I first read *Think and Grow Rich*. I realized that I had stopped short of the ultimate goal I had set for myself after I left home at 12. I would seek not just relative success but extraordinary success that would be part of an extraordinary life.

The show ended. I knew that I wanted to emulate Khashoggi, achieving at least his level of success, and the only way to do so was to work and learn directly from him. I turned to my guests and said, "One day soon I will be working with Adnan Khashoggi." After a brief silence, a few of them chuckled, then in different ways that all amounted to the same negative point, told me straight up that I didn't have a chance.

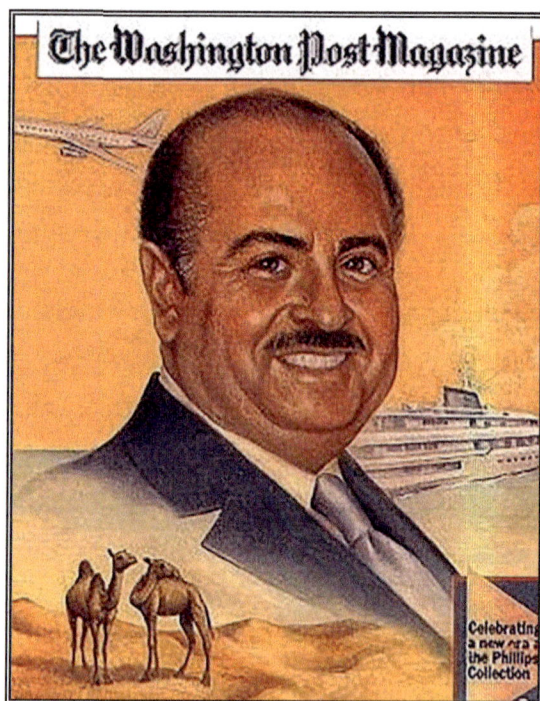

*Detail from a Washington Post Magazine cover with the headline "Adnan Khashoggi: Inside the Fantasy World of a Saudi Billionaire."*

Whether the negative influences are from friends or foes, you must, as *Think and Grow Rich* urges, insulate yourself so that you can move forward. I didn't argue with my guests or become angry. Instead, I recycled their criticisms into fuel for my new burning desire.

This was going to be the biggest challenge I had ever undertaken. I decided to read *Think and Grow Rich* again that night so that I could refresh in my mind the principles that I had been using automatically my entire life. I had strayed off the path, becoming complacent, too comfortable with my achievements. After watching what Khashoggi had achieved in his life, I realized that I needed to recalibrate my whole life.

### Burning All My Ships.

*Think and Grow Rich* discusses a warrior's battle strategy, one that gave me the foresight to never give up and to put myself in a position so that success would be the only alternative.

> Long ago, a great warrior faced a situation that made it necessary for him to make a decision that insured his success on the battlefield. He was about to send his armies against a powerful foe, whose men outnumbered his own. He loaded his soldiers into boats, sailed to the enemy's country, unloaded soldiers and equipment, then gave the order to burn the ships that had carried them. Addressing the men before the first battle, he said, "You see the boats going up in smoke. That means that we cannot leave these shores unless we win! We now have no choice—*we win or we perish!*"

I decided to use the warrior's strategy: I had to burn my ships. I went about the next few weeks selling everything I had at a fire-sale pace, receiving one tenth of the value of my assets. At the end, I was now free to search out, and learn from, the richest man in the world. I refused to be manipulated by the fear of poverty, just as I had refused to be manipulated by the fear of criticism from my guests after the TV show.

I had to shift and move forward if I was going to achieve not just success, but the success of an extraordinary life.

*More is lost through indecision than the wrong decision.*

### Reading the Cards.

I went through every contact, and then contacts of contacts all over the world in an attempt to find someone who knew Khashoggi personally and might provide access (my current contacts number over 7,000, most of which allow me to call directly). After a full year of trying, I located a professional "psychic" who read tarot cards and had been introduced to Khashoggi through his driver. I asked for an introduction to the driver, but also gave the psychic $10,000 so that the next time he read

the cards he would "see" a man named Ramy who would appear some day in the future.

Then I asked the driver to introduce me to staff members and others who constantly surrounded Khashoggi, such as his lawyers and even his chiropractor, a network I pursued for another six months so that my name would be consistently on the radar.

You might wonder whether I subverted all these people, somehow turned them into my own double-agents and away from Khashoggi. But that's not how I operate at all. Instead, part of the trust I developed included the sincere belief that I ultimately was working in Khashoggi's best interest, that I was completely on his side. If I hadn't been confident and convincing on this point, that network would have fallen apart. I made sure to protect their identities and confidence, and they protected mine as well.

*Trust is gained by working in others' best interests.*

## Stacking the Deck in My Favor.

Nearly two years after my decision to relentlessly pursue Khashoggi, my plan paid off: He was going to be in New York (where he owned two floors on top of the Olympic Tower), and he invited me to come for tea. I arrived two hours early, so I sat on the steps of the nearby St. Patrick's Cathedral, contemplating how to approach the richest man in the world and then convince him to let me work alongside him.

## Patience and Opportunity.

Reflecting on *Think and Grow Rich* again, I remembered one of the stories that Hill related about Edwin C. Barnes, who wanted to become a business associate of Thomas Edison. He hopped on a train, presented himself, and just informed Edison that he was going to be working with him. In Barnes's case, Edison saw something in him—his definiteness of purpose—and decided to let the man work with him.

Barnes waited patiently for the right opportunity. When Edison invented an electric dictating machine, Barnes was up to the challenge, successfully selling the Ediphone and making millions with the great inventor. I thought, *If it worked for Barnes, it can work for me.*

---

Successful people are decisive people. When opportunities come their way, they evaluate them carefully, make a decision, and take appropriate action. They know that indecision wastes time that could be spent on more productive tasks.

—*Think and Grow Rich*

Though I don't act randomly, I also don't spend time obsessing over *whether* to act. Indecision, as *Think and Grow Rich* teaches, is itself a kind of action, but one that wastes time and resources.

∧⁄

At the appointed time, I stepped out of the elevator and into his apartment. The lavish appointments initially dazzled me, a palace-like interior which even now would be difficult to describe with just words, but I instantly revised the way I saw life and the attainment of immense wealth. Such wealth was no longer just an abstract concept but instead a concrete reality. If one man who also started with nothing could achieve that kind of success, there was no reason why I could not do so myself.

After about 15 minutes, Khashoggi—I already had begun to think of him as "Adnan"—walked down a spiral staircase, paused, looked at me, and said, "Aah, Ramy!" The richest man in the world knew my name! He offered me something to drink, and I nervously requested a Coca-Cola, which he proceeded to pour into a glass.

We sat down in one of his many living rooms, and after some small talk, he asked what I currently was doing and what I was looking to do in the future. I knew that this was my chance to implement the Barnes principle. I informed Khashoggi that I not only would be working with him but would be the best person who ever worked with him, careful to emphasize the word *with* rather than *for*.

 *Work with others, not for others.*

Khashoggi laughed a little, then stopped when he saw that I was serious. He dismissed the whole idea, emphasizing that he was much too busy, and said that I should return in a few years. No doubt many people would have given up at that point, but I made a counteroffer of a week, after which I would present him with a deal so impressive that it would prove my worth to him. He accepted my offer out of sheer politeness, I thought, but the essential point was that *he accepted*.

When you apply your faith in yourself, the result is a positive course of
action that when persistently followed will almost always lead to success. When you believe in your ideas
and in your abilities, and you trust in
the Infinite Intelligence of the universe, you know that your thoughts
and deeds will ultimately lead to a successful conclusion. You cannot fail.

—*Think and Grow Rich*

— REFLECTION —

I always have faith in myself, which is
an essential trait for success.

## Let's Make a Deal.

I returned to Tampa with absolutely no clue about what I could bring back to Adnan. I needed to perform some quick, focused, relevant research (there was not yet a public internet). As was (and is) my habit, I made notes and brainstormed from the moment I left Adnan, and by the time my plane landed, I realized that I could go to my brokerage house and read through S&P sheets, which I proceeded to do, combing through company after company until I found one that appeared extremely undervalued.

I flew back to New York, excited to present a strong deal to a man I had come to idolize, but when I arrived, to my dismay I was shunted to one of his assistants who barely paid attention to my presentation. I asked to see Adnan, and the assistant blandly replied that he was busy.

Without a word, I stood up and proceeded to search the apartment for Adnan, whom I found sitting quietly in one of his many rooms. After I sat down, I said that I understood why I was being brushed off since countless people no doubt approached him with various deals. I understood that I was only 27 years old, yet I would be the best person he had ever worked with.

Adnan again insisted that he was busy and that I should come back in a few years. But I had internalized the principles of *Think and Grow Rich* and had ignited a new burning desire. I was sitting close to a model of an extraordinary life, and I knew that my future path would include Adnan.

There was no way back—I had burned all of my ships.

When you are actively working toward a goal, there are no failures; there are only degrees of success. Take the initiative. When you are faced with a problem or a difficult decision, don't waste endless hours agonizing over the solution. If you analyze the situation objectively, you will always find an answer. Don't focus on the problem; focus on the solution. Then get into action.

*—Think and Grow Rich*

— REFLECTION —

I stopped thinking about situations as presenting "problems." Instead, I constantly sketch out potential solutions without initially worrying about practicality. I learned to trust my creative process.

## Planning and Maneuvering.

To reach my goal of working directly with Adnan, I needed to use what I already had accomplished. Part of my process is to continually take an inventory of my current assets, especially my human capital. I already had encountered too many people who failed to tally what they truly possessed, and, if they realized a deficit in their network or in their character, failed to immediately fill the gaps. We should train ourselves to ask, "What do I have that I can deploy strategically?" and not "What do I lack?"

I lacked all sorts of items at various times in my life, but in the spirit of *Think and Grow Rich*, I didn't spend any appreciable time worrying about what I didn't have. As military leaders often remind us, we have to fight with the resources we actually possess right now.

*Constantly inventory your true assets, even if it is just a single burning desire.*

Having developed a powerful network of Adnan contacts, I talked with four people who were particularly close to him, offering each $10,000 per month if they updated me on his location. I promised to never betray their trust, a promise I have kept to this day. (I'll reiterate what I said earlier: I would not be successful if my approach was to encourage betrayal. Instead, my success is built on others' realization that I am a trustworthy ally, in this case, of Adnan. I can't guarantee that other people won't try to betray *my* trust, but my own reputation will remain intact, as yours should if you wish to create an honorable business and personal life.)

After I was informed of what would be Adnan's next location after he left New York, I headed to the Hôtel Le Bristol in Paris. From the airport I went directly to the hotel, found the general manager, and confidently told him I was Adnan's advance man, tasked with making sure all of his rooms were arranged satisfactorily after which I would help check him in.

The general manager quickly assured me that all was correctly arranged, and invited me to relax before Adnan's arrival.

After a few hours, Adnan strolled into the lobby, then stopped, astonished at my presence. Without skipping a beat, I stepped up close, telling him that had I set up everything according to his wishes. He said nothing and instead just followed the valet to his room.

To accomplish anything worthwhile often requires years. But knowledge alone is not power; it becomes powerful only when it is applied through positive action. Study after study of successful people reveals that they have a bias for action. They gather the appropriate facts, relate them to their knowledge, develop an implementation plan, and then get into action. When in doubt, it's far better to act too soon rather than too late.

—*Think and Grow Rich*

— REFLECTION —

My acting quickly and decisively did not give me a reputation for being impulsive. Instead, I built a reputation for getting things done.

### Useful but Not Intrusive.

The next stop was London, and again I flew ahead, went to his hotel, and arranged everything. I kept this up, making myself available to him for anything he required. He started to become accustomed to my presence, and I kept on finding new ways to make myself useful without being overly intrusive.

I would always rent the next-best suite in whatever hotel he stayed in, positioning myself as an equal and not an employee. I persisted in my pursuit for another year and a half, until I was completely out of money and owed $85,000 on my American Express card.

The situation might have seemed dire to others, but I recast it as an *opportunity*. "Let me work on one deal," I said to Adnan one day, "and if I make the deal better than you expect, I will work with you from then on. If I fail to do so, I will leave, and you will never have to see me again." He thought about it, noting that I had been around a while and had paid my dues. He decided to give me one chance.

*When I turned a No into a Yes.*

He outlined a deal he wanted to structure, and I accepted the challenge. The years at his side had not been wasted: I watched him closely, learning the whole time. I was more than prepared to pull off the deal.

The resulting deal was a far better one than he had asked for. I had impressed him, and from that day forward, I was at his side constantly, structuring deals across the world. Our experiences and accomplishments could fill a dozen books, but the real message for me was never giving up if I wanted to achieve an extraordinary goal along the way to an extraordinary life.

Most failures could have been converted into successes if someone had held on another minute or made more effort. When you have the potential for success within you, adversity and temporary defeat only help you prepare to reach great heights of success. Without adversity, you would never develop the qualities of reliability, loyalty, humility, and perseverance that are so essential to enduring success. Many people have escaped the jaws of defeat and achieved great victories because they would not allow themselves to fail. When your escape routes are all closed, you will be surprised how quickly you will find the path to success.

—*Think and Grow Rich*

Once I decided to close off my possible "escape routes," my default thinking shifted so that I never again even considered those possibilities.

# CHAPTER 5:

## RELOCATING AND REBALANCING

O ver the seven years I spent with Adnan, I learned more than just how to structure complex business transactions.

I also came to better understand the world and the people in it, as well as the richness of different economic and political cultures. I learned to adapt to whatever situation I faced and what it meant to move on the world stage. Most important, my thinking had risen to an entirely new, powerful level.

I never stopped admiring Adnan as a person. Now that he is gone, there are negative stories and voices, as well as extremely positive ones, about his life and business. I only can say that I never have lost faith in his essential integrity and overall decent nature. Once you're gone, you can't control your own story anymore, but to this day, Adnan remains an inspiration in my daily life.

*Thinking About What Matters.*

Before I met Adnan, though I was a millionaire, a billion dollars—
let alone billions of dollars—was a vague concept at best. After the
time I spent with him and many other billionaires, it became an everyday way of thinking, a reality, and something that I knew I could
achieve. I was now in my early 30s and ready to take the next, crucial
steps.

Doctors are doctors because they study medicine, read medical jour-
nals, take care of patients, and keep up with the latest medical ad-
vances. They think about their role as doctors most of the time, and
not necessarily about new business opportunities for creating stratospheric wealth.

The same holds true of any profession, from engineers to lawyers to
chefs: You truly become what you think about most of the time,
which is why I constantly think about building wealth. This book so
far has demonstrated that habit, if no other: The desire has to con-
sume your waking thoughts but in a way that is energizing and not
destructive. Just as I can recognize opportunities that present themselves to me, you should place yourself in the same, constant state of
mind.

You will never be greater than the thoughts that dominate your mind. If it's true that you become what you think about most, it follows that the quantity and quality of success you achieve in your life will be in direct proportion to the size of your thoughts. If you allow your mind to be dominated by trivial matters, your achievements are likely to be unimportant. Discipline yourself to think about important things. Keep up with what's new in your field and with what's going on in the world. Make a list of good ideas that you can use anytime you are searching for a creative solution to a problem. Remember, small minds think about things; great minds think about ideas.

—*Think and Grow Rich*

I keep reflecting on *Think and Grow Rich* since I want my mind to be large, expansive, and powerful. I refuse to let my mind to be chained to small matters and small ideas.

We all have potentially great ideas, but the one quality that really separates the people who succeed from the ones who don't is not hesitating to execute those ideas or take advantage of opportunities. Over and over again, people who succeed are the ones who don't let indecision cripple them and instead just take action.

*We all have at least one great idea, but it is useless without decisive action.*

It's worth mentioning again that more is lost through indecision than through a wrong decision. I would rather make many wrong decisions and shift and correct them as needed than debate every decision endlessly until the opportunity passes me by. If you have anchored yourself with a burning desire for an extraordinary life, you will find the decisions that you make correctly will far outnumber the wrong decisions. And those decisions are what propel you to achieve any worthwhile goal.

I finally reached a point where, though it had been an honor to be called "Khashoggi's guy," I had learned enough to go out on own. It was time to shift to the next level.

After years of traveling the world, I decided to make Los Angeles my home base. Los Angeles to me was—and is—everything I was looking for to create an extraordinary life. From 12 to 33, I was laser-focused, moving from one level of success to the next. Now it was time, I thought, to rebalance my life between work and play, not to mention romance.

### *A Jet Is Never Just a Jet.*

I remember vividly the first time I boarded one of Khashoggi's planes, a fully-customized, private DC-9 Aircraft. When I walked on that plane, I thought, *One day I will own a plane exactly like this one.* When I arrived in LA, I quickly located a private DC-9 for sale. The day I bought the plane, I stood outside just looking at it for an hour.

I had heard of people crying from joy, but this was the first time I actually did so. The plane was more than just exceptional transportation: It was a marker of how I had reached the goals I had so far set for myself. I looked around and realized that I had achieved precisely what I had set out to achieve.

In the philosophy of *Think and Grow Rich*, the plane symbolized the maxim that *whatever our minds can conceive can be achieved*. Even though the plane would bring my friends, business associates, and me great pleasure, I still never forgot the strategic power of certain acquisitions.

If you are going to move past the city level to the state level, or past the state to the national arena or on to the international stage, your lifestyle signals just what sort of deals you can broker. There is no consumption for consumption's sake—you can enjoy the fruits of your labor while also keeping an eye on strategic necessity and efficiency. I never think that I can't live without some material object, since, as happened to me later when I again lost my fortune, I might have to do without some or all of my possessions.

*The Hollywood Playground.*

*With Hugh Hefner and his physician, Mark Saginor.*

In Los Angeles in 1994, I approached play with the same focus as business: I would become both a regular at the Playboy Mansion and a Hollywood insider.

I was young and thoroughly enjoyed the parties and altogether lavish entertainments of the jetsetters. Just as I had intended, I became a regular guest at the Mansion and attended A-list Hollywood functions.

Famous actors constantly are pestered by people who ask them for something. To break into Hollywood in a more elegant manner, I made sure that I was known as someone who never asked directly for anything. Instead, I was the person who donated, hosted events, or took others with me to Las Vegas and many other parts of the world on memorable trips.

I built an important new reputation as someone who wouldn't just attend a charity auction—I would bid up so that the item unquestionably would come to me, and then I usually gave the item back. I was so well known for this behavior that if an item wasn't attracting bidders, the auctioneer would just default to the "Ramy Bid."

*With actor Kirstie Alley at one of her charity events.*

### Turning a No to a Yes.

After my years with Adnan, I came across John Gray's *Men Are From Mars, Women Are From Venus* and was struck by its potential for helping me better understand and communicate with women. After reading the book, I was intrigued enough to buy tickets for his next personal seminar.

I was thoroughly impressed by John's pure genius and insight, and when the seminar was over, I approached and said that I wanted to represent him, market his books and teaching, and create multiple revenue streams. John politely and firmly declined. He said that many people constantly approached him, and some of them were very experienced and could do a much better job than I could, especially since I was new to this level of marketing.

I engineered a dinner invitation with John and his wife, and by dessert had convinced him to let me be his representative. Before accepting, he mentioned the well-known, highly-competitive marketing firms that were vying to represent his work. The dinner became a compressed version of my dogged pursuit of Adnan, and to that relentless attitude I added a sincere belief in the power of John's work to transform people's lives.

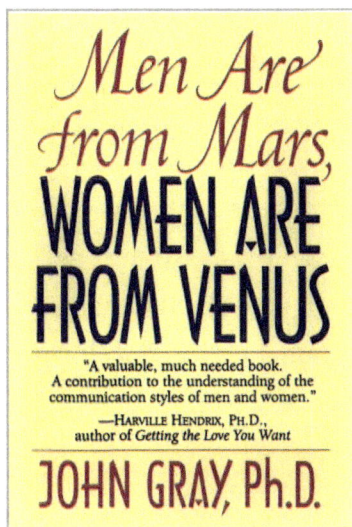

*Men Are from Mars,* WOMEN ARE FROM VENUS

"A valuable, much needed book. A contribution to the understanding of the communication styles of men and women."

—Harville Hendrix, Ph.D., author of *Getting the Love You Want*

JOHN GRAY, Ph.D.

I didn't tell him how he needed to change or tweak his vision. Instead, I placed myself inside his vision, finally convincing him that I wouldn't give up no matter what happened. I transformed a firm *No* to a *Yes.*

 *Find the yes behind the no.*

I have discovered that there is *always* a yes behind every no. Every time I changed a no to a yes, I gained more confidence I could do so again, just as *Think and Grow Rich* advises that all the little victories will provide the confidence for achieving the big victories. And the more you test the principles and see that they work, the more confidence you have that they will work every time.

Turning a no into a yes is not overwhelming or unfairly manipulating someone else. Just as *Think and Grow Rich* equates the "Master Mind" to a "spirit of harmony, between two or more people, for the attainment of a definite purpose," you are powerfully persuasive when you demonstrate that you are attuned to someone else's best interests.

I have been testing every one of those principles now for over 40 years. They have never failed me, and they have become fused into my psyche.

### The Genesis of an Idea.

I started the Genesis media group as a company to market John's work—as well as all the future personalities and products that I would discover—with the goal of building Genesis into a billion-dollar company. I also kept up a business relationship with Adnan, who was a big investor in my company.

My first task in building John's further success was to produce a series of videos from the dozen seminars he gave, then create an infomercial to sell those videos. The infomercial alone was responsible for hundreds of millions of dollars in revenue and drove the purchase of more than 50 million books. *Men Are From Mars, Woman Are From Venus* became a runaway hardback bestseller, staying at number one on the *New York Times* best-seller list for five years and outselling, except for The Bible, any other book at the time.

John was a visionary, and I supported not just eventual greater success, but also the opportunity to make his ideas part of our everyday culture. If something didn't work, I just retooled the campaign until it did, without taking any of the profits, and to John's credit, he rode out the inevitable ups and downs, remaining focused on the horizon. His personal faith in me would reappear later when it was sorely needed.

*Working with John Gray on set.*

After the success of John's marketing, I added a profitable line of new programs, changed the company's name to GenesisIntermedia, and took it public. GenesisIntermedia—on track to become a potential multibillion-dollar company not just through the products that we marketed but also through our demonstrated marketing skills—was retooled as a business "incubator" that started or acquired other companies and built them up so that they eventually could be spun off as their own independent, public companies.

PROSPECTUS
June 14, 1999

GENESIS
INTERMEDIA

GENESIS MEDIA GROUP

# GENESISINTERMEDIA.COM, INC.
## 2,000,000 SHARES OF COMMON STOCK

We are a marketing company that markets our own products and our clients' products utilizing conventional media and interactive multimedia technologies. The underwriters named in this prospectus are initially offering the stock in the United States and internationally on a firm commitment basis at a price of $8.50 per share. All of the common stock being offered is being sold by us.

This is our initial public offering and prior to this offering no public market existed for our stock. Our stock has been approved for listing on the Pacific Exchange under the symbol GNS and has been approved for quotation on the Nasdaq National Market under the symbol GENI.

*This investment involves a high degree of risk and could result in a loss of your investment. See "Risk Factors" beginning on page 7.*

|  | Per Share | Total |
| --- | --- | --- |
| • Price to the Public | $8.50 | $17,000,000 |
| • Underwriting Discounts and Commissions | $ .68 | $ 1,360,000 |
| • Proceeds to Genesis | $7.82 | $15,640,000 |

The table does not include a three percent (3%) non-accountable expense allowance payable to the underwriters. The underwriters may purchase an additional 300,000 shares solely to cover over-allotments.

*Neither the Securities and Exchange Commission nor any state securities commission has approved or disapproved these securities, or determined if this prospectus is truthful or complete. Any representation to the contrary is a criminal offense.*

## MILLENNIUM FINANCIAL GROUP, INC.
## HD BROUS & CO., INC.
### AMERICAN FRONTEER FINANCIAL CORPORATION

My investors were rewarded with an exponential 1,000% increase in the stock value over just two years. I eventually brought the market capitalization of GenesisIntermedia to $1 billion.

# CHAPTER 6:

## FLYING WITH ICAHN

M y new ventures involved buying and developing companies with strong potential as well as starting new ones.

I am energized by the creativity needed to build up rather than tear
down, and wove this feature into the production of great wealth.

*Focus on what you and others can build.*

In order to scale up, I found people who could become expert managers, mentoring them so that they in turn could build successful
companies. I continue to value focus and tenacity. The intricacies of
business transactions can be learned, but my most trusted associates

display their own burning desire to succeed in life, a desire that must be clearly demonstrated every single day.

*Travel opportunities.*

### Refusing to Get Lost.

After buying Global Leisure Travel, a conglomerate of many travel companies, I read an article about how the billionaire Carl Icahn was taking the company LowestFare.com public. LowestFair.com had about the same valuation as Global Leisure Travel, and I immediately recognized an important opportunity: I would be able to cash out of Global Leisure Travel in a big way if I could convince Icahn to merge the two companies.

I started analyzing how I could obtain access to Icahn. I had never spoken to him and had no immediate secondary contact, either. He had a well-known reputation for being prickly and just plain difficult. I took an inventory of what I did know at the time:

1. At the time, Icahn was involved in the purchase of the Stratosphere Hotel and Casino in Las Vegas.

2. He would visit Vegas to see his purchase.

3. While in Vegas, he would stay at a much more luxurious hotel than the Stratosphere.

I offered my usual casino hosts in Vegas, which I visited frequently during this time for both pleasure and business, a large finder's fee for the one who would tell me where he was staying.

One of the hosts came through: Icahn was booked into a villa at the Las Vegas Hilton, which happened also to be one of my favorite places to stay. I immediately booked the villa right next to his.

I arrived in Vegas on the same day as Icahn. I knew that he would go to dinner around 7 pm—which was another detail I had gleaned from my host—so at 6:30 I knocked on his door. Icahn opened the door, swore loudly, and demanded to know who I was.

I replied calmly and pleasantly that I was the guy he would do the next business deal with, and before I could say more, he glowered and told me to get lost since he was on his way to dinner. I said that dinner would be perfect since I hadn't eaten, then grabbed my date (whom I had brought along on purpose) and followed him to the elevator.

During the ride down to the lobby, he cursed at me nonstop, with only brief pauses to call me crazy. Once outside the hotel, I dashed with my date ahead of him and jumped right into his limo, after which he continued to curse at me throughout the ride, while walking into the restaurant, and even after being seated. I suspected that, in spite of the name-calling and apparent anger, he wanted to see how the evening would play out. I never stopped smiling.

In our later work together, I came to understand that he didn't generally encounter people he couldn't immediately intimidate into backing down. As desert arrived, he finally ran out of curses and lapsed into at least mild curiosity. I offered him a ride back on my plane, which was larger and more luxurious than the one he had chartered, but, in keeping with his established style, he said he didn't give a damn about my owning a plane.

Our dinner finished, we rode straight to the airport and parked in front of my plane. (I had secretly paid the driver to take us directly there.) Icahn grumbled a bit, said, "What the hell," and consented to a tour, after which he admitted that it was a fine plane. He also emphasized that he could buy thousands of them, and that he still didn't want a ride. We drove back to the hotel.

On the day of Icahn's departure, he arrived at the airport, expecting to board his privately-chartered flight, but—mysteriously—his plane hadn't arrived as scheduled. I had checked out of the hotel earlier and arranged to have my plane fueled and ready, so naturally I strolled over and offered Icahn a ride, which he accepted after his usual grumbling.

We talked for the next six and a half hours, during which Icahn told me about himself, including some details about where he lived and how he worked. When we landed, he said, true to form, "Get lost—I never want to see you again." I laughed.

*Conversations always are opportunities to learn about and align visions.*

### The Pursuit Continues.

Carl—this was how I would think of him since, as with Khashoggi, I wasn't an employee but his equal—had given me enough information to find one of his residences in the Hamptons. I headed to Carl's home and arrived at his door at 7 am on a Friday. When his maid answered, I confidently told her that I was Carl's guest and asked if she could show me to my room.

After pretending to settle in for a few minutes, I left the room and found the breakfast table on the outside patio, where I waited with a cup of coffee. Carl came downstairs for his usual breakfast, and after spotting me, yelled that he would call the police. I sat quietly and smiled for a moment, then told him to relax and that he wasn't going to call the police. I said to have a cup of coffee.

Carl finally calmed down and sat to have some coffee. I stayed with him through the weekend, followed him to New York, and then returned with him the weekend after. The whole time, he kept telling me to get lost, and I kept finding creative ways to stay around him. Eventually, he bought a large slice of Global Leisure Travel.

*Playing poker in New York with Carl Icahn.*

Over the next few years, we worked on more deals, including a $100 million line of credit to GenesisIntermedia for acquisitions. He never dropped his habit of cursing at me.

*With Carl and Gail Icahn.*

# CHAPTER 7:

## BETTING AGAINST ME

A company that is public also is a target for investors who bet against it by shorting the stock.

Inevitably, as you invest yourself and your reputation in a company, you come to see short-sellers as people who bet directly against *you*, hoping that you'll fail.

As I grew the valuation of GenesisIntermedia, I noticed an unusually large position accumulating on the short side, almost 7,000,000 shares. Short-selling is just a fact of the investment landscape, but this seemed like a signal of a direct attack, and one that now engaged my full attention. I don't like anyone betting against me, especially since I had proved that those who did would lose in the long run.

## Battling the Shorts.

I created a clear, burning desire to not just *battle* the shorts but to *beat* them as well. The short-sellers, it seemed to me, intended to damage the stock's value, and by doing so would damage my investors and associates. Eventually, I found out about unethical tactics that some of the short-sellers employed.

*Educate yourself about the challenges you encounter.*

I set about learning everything there was to know about the mechanisms and legal rules that short-sellers have to follow. To short a stock legally, you have to first borrow the stock from someone, for example, a brokerage firm. Once you borrow the shares, you can sell those shares to establish a short position. The short-sellers' general plan is to buy back the shares at a lower price.

My own plan was straightforward: I would block the short-sellers' ability to borrow the stock. I let everyone in my wide-ranging network know about the short position, and enlisted those who believed in the stock to buy more. This time, however, I urged them to put in their cash accounts or ask for the stock in physical form, thus removing the stock from accounts from which it could be borrowed. The short-sellers would have a difficult time establishing a larger short position.

But the short position kept increasing. Short-sellers were starting to illegally short the stock, I found, by not even trying to borrow the stock—they just kept on shorting.

A few people, including Adnan, kept on buying the stock until we owned 140% of what was available. (Though it may seem odd that more of a company can be owned than is available, when people sell stock they don't own, this situation can occur.) Knowing that the stock was oversold, I started asking for delivery. By law, the stock needed to be delivered within three days.

The short-sellers kept failing to deliver the stock because they didn't own it. When someone can't deliver stock, the brokerage firm that initiated the sale is responsible. The firm will be forced to go into the open market every three days and buy it in the last half hour for whatever can be had. The short-sellers, not wanting the price to rise, would resell into that buying, moving deeper and deeper into the short position while the stock price continued to climb.

The short-sellers, who were losing hundreds of millions of dollars while shorting my stock, were desperate. They tried tarnishing my reputation and even threatened my life. Their last-ditch effort was lodging a complaint with the SEC in so that the government would initiate an investigation. The short-sellers hoped that I would be forced to announce the investigation, thus damaging the stock.

### Committed to the Fight.

The battle would turn into the biggest challenge in my life to that point, one that, if I lost, would mean facing 100 years in jail. Just as important was protecting my reputation that I had worked so hard to build among my investors and associates.

I was committed to fighting the short-sellers with the financial resources I had gained in the years since I applied the lessons of *Think and Grow Rich*, but then something happened that I never could have predicted: 911. Nothing compares to the agony that the victims and their families endured, of course. But the two-week market shutdown followed by the collapse of stocks because of fear had the side effect of emboldening the short-sellers.

My own stock also collapsed, but the difference between my situation and others is that I had an Arab name, which now drew suspicion. Adnan Khashoggi—a Saudi who was labeled an arms dealer by the tabloid press—owned 40% of the company. We became immediate targets for the government (I was to learn later to what extent the short-sellers had a hand in what was going to happen). My stock was halted, and I lost all my net worth in a single day.

### The Seven-Year Battle.

For the next seven years, I fought the US government's attempt to indict me on completely unfounded, false allegations. Without my primary commitment to never giving up, I would have gone to jail— as the prosecutor told me, the government wins 98% of such cases.

The government offered me many deals, ranging from 4 to 7 years in jail, as opposed to over 100 years if I went to court and lost. But I refused to make any deal, even though others who were innocent have done so to avoid the worst-case scenario. I, following the principles of *Think and Grow Rich*, set my mind on winning what was now the most important challenge of my life: securing my innocence and reputation.

I refused to be swayed the possible loss of my freedom, an alibi of the sort that *Think and Grow Rich* warns us to discard. I was determined to prove my innocence and head off even an indictment. However, because I had devoted 100% of my resources to the fight against the short-sellers, I also had lost my fortune, which meant that I had to start over once again while battling the scurrilous charges. And here is the price tag for fighting an unjust set of allegations: 20 million dollars.

Nearly every day for seven years, I sent my attorneys to the prosecutors' office, where they meticulously walked through the weaknesses in the allegations. The prosecutors would relent on one point, then push another theory, hoping to bring an indictment before a grand jury, but my lawyers every time would pinpoint weaknesses that would fatally compromise the government's case.

In such cases, defendants or potential defendants have very few advantages. The government can wield its power in a threatening way: For example, a close associate of mine was indicted in order to provide leverage, a possible witness who might "turn." Courtney Smith—someone I consider a good friend—faced 40 years in jail if he lost. But he knew we had done nothing wrong and was not going to lie, even though he faced such a harsh possible outcome.

After a long trial involving both the Department of Justice and the SEC, he was acquitted on all counts. The government also lost another potential weapon to use against me.

*Adversity is never permanent.*

*Expect Setbacks and Move Forward.*

No matter how carefully you study a subject, no matter how rationally you make decisions, no matter how well-prepared you are, you will occasionally make mistakes, as well as encounter unexpected or unpredictable events. But temporary setbacks—even seven-year ones—are not permanent failures. Successful people recognize that we all experience temporary setbacks that require us to reevaluate our performance and take corrective action to achieve success. They know that adversity is never permanent.

The mind is a more powerful weapon than any yet invented, one that cannot be completely controlled or contained by an outside force, however formidable that force may at first appear. Throughout history, tyrants have tried to control those who opposed them, but eventually these rulers discovered that the power of the imagination was far greater than the threat of the sword. As Victor Hugo said, "An invasion of armies can be resisted, but not an idea whose time has come."

Though I haven't discussed the imagination directly, you can tell that the possibilities for creating an extraordinary life appear when I can let my imagination run free, employing what *Think and Grow Rich* calls the "workshop of the mind." When that imagination was later muzzled for a while, I drifted off the path that I had set for myself.

You can use my example for your own: Do not let any sort of tyrant, any negative influence, control you. You can learn something valuable from the harshest of situations, rather than let pain, disappointment, and outrage extinguish your creative imagination.

*If you can control your own mind, you will never be controlled by the mind of another.*

### Never Giving Up.

My lawyers were able to obtain transcripts of FBI witness interviews, many of which contained clear inconsistencies, and then convince the office of the prosecutor to re-interview a number of witnesses. The new testimony showed even further inconsistencies.

In a last-ditch effort, the prosecutors, who clearly saw the writing on the wall, offered a final deal: Take 4 years or face a possible 100 years.

I refused since I had done nothing wrong. That deal was offered on a Tuesday, and when my attorneys called me on Thursday, I was convinced that I had been indicted. Instead, they had received a letter from the office of the prosecutor that the case was being dropped (one of my attorneys has seen such a letter only once before in his entire career). I asked my attorneys to repeat that statement five times. Clearly, the prosecutors knew they had no real case.

U. S. Department of Justice

*United States Attorney*
*Central District of California*

Stephen A. Cazares
Assistant United States Attorney
(213) 894-0707 (o)
(213) 894-6269 (f)

United States Courthouse
312 North Spring Street
Los Angeles, California 90012

August 2, 2007

**VIA FAX & U.S. MAIL**

Tom Pollack, Esq.
Irell & Manella LLP
1800 Avenue of the Stars, Suite 900
Los Angeles, CA 90067

      Re:   Ramy El-Batrawi

Dear Mr. Pollack:

      This letter serves to notify you that, based on the information presently known to it, the United States Attorney's Office for the Central District of California ("USAO") is declining to prosecute your client, Ramy El-Batrawi ("Mr. El-Batrawi"), for alleged criminal violations arising out of (1) stock loans related to shares of GenesisIntermedia.com, Inc.; (2) trading in GenesisIntermedia.com, Inc. stock; and (3) any false representations in filings with the Securities and Exchange Commission in relation to GenesisIntermdia.com, Inc., all in the time period June 1999 through September 2001.

      Notwithstanding the foregoing, should additional information come to the USAO's attention regarding the alleged violations described above, the USAO retains the right to alter its position and proceed with prosecution of Mr. El-Batrawi. Please be advised, however, that this declination letter does not affect or bind the USAO with respect to its ability to prosecute Mr. El-Batrawi for any other unlawful past or future conduct.

      Very truly yours,

GEORGE S. CARDONA
United States Attorney

STEPHEN A. CAZARES
Assistant United States Attorney
Major Frauds Section

After seven years, I had won the battle, though I never learned what had precisely motivated the government to finally admit defeat. I did learn that the case was initiated before 911 when a group of short-sellers paid an FBI agent to claim to the SEC that I had engaged in various forms of fraud. Three FBI agents that were involved ended up being indicted for their actions, and two of them, along with one of the short-sellers, went to jail (I wasn't exaggerating earlier when I mentioned death threats, either.)

*Victory is always possible for the person who refuses to stop fighting.*

The news always focused on my being sued by the SEC, not the rest of this disgraceful case. Such negative press—spread easily because of the internet—could have been an alibi for not succeeding. Many people simply refused to do business with me during this period and after, but I refused to be cowed in any way. I continued to approach everyone with confidence, convincing them that they should be skeptical of what they read.

I would spend years fighting to regain everything that I had lost.

If you think you are beaten, you are, if you think you dare not, you don't. If you like to win, but you think you can't, it is almost certain you won't. If you think you'll lose, you're lost. For out of the world we find, Success begins with a person's will—it's all in the state of mind. If you think you are outclassed, you are, you've got to think high to rise. You've got to be sure of yourself before you can ever win a prize. Life's battles don't always go to the stronger or faster man but soon or late the one who wins is the one WHO THINKS HE CAN! (from the poem by Walter D. Wintle).

—*Think and Grow Rich*

When I started to slip into a negative mindset, which *Think and Grow Rich* warns against, I knew that I had to take action. If I didn't, I would lose future battles.

Even with the constant, everyday battle with the government, I still managed to put together deals and build solid trust, though the physical and psychological strain was extraordinary. I offered $18 billion to buy Universal studios, and then cornered the industrialist Marvin Davis at Spago's, where I had learned he always ate lunch, for a $4 billion commitment as an anchor investor, after which I put together another 14 billion from multiple investors and banks. (The whole deal collapsed when Davis tried to pull off his own deal behind my back and made a premature announcement to the press. The deal ultimately was lost to NBC.) But the takeaway here is that no deal is too big.

Some of my other projects included the Piccadilly chain of 300 cafeterias (the very restaurant that I had eaten in when I was homeless and living on the streets), and two airlines, Aloha and Era, the latter based out of Alaska.

Because of the ongoing legal fights, I chose to remain in the background. I did not control the companies I purchased with investors, but instead let other people make the daily operational decisions. Unfortunately, those in charge—even an accomplished billionaire—often did not share the same principles of success, and both Piccadilly and Aloha filed for bankruptcy, while Era sold at a break-even price.

My new commitment was to never again be involved in any business that I did not control at the outset. I understood how to identify and nurture leadership, an important topic in *Think and Grow Rich*, so if I needed to turn operations over to someone, that person would have the character traits that would ensure success.

*All failures are temporary.*

### Imagination Grounded.

I now was completely broke again and had to find a way to build wealth. While I was battling the government, a psychiatrist had convinced me that I should take antidepressants, among other medications, to combat the constant stress, claiming that doing so was the only way I would be able to handle the situation.

Gradually, my thought processes slowed down. My previous ability to imagine new projects, something that was as natural as breathing to me, just disappeared. I was operating at a fraction of my mental capacity. I seemed to have fallen into a deep hole from which I could find no way to climb back out.

I seemed to be trapped in a cycle of medications, and to even consider that possibility was foreign since it sounded too much like an alibi. According to the psychiatrist, it would be dangerous for me to stop or go cold turkey, since the physical and mental side effects—the latter including potential suicidal thoughts—were just too severe.

Even though he recommended a possible program of gradual tapering off, he somehow never thought I was quite ready. I was 53 years old, broke, hooked on prescription drugs, and clueless about my next step.

No action takes place unless it is preceded by thought. If you're unhappy with the circumstances in which you find yourself, you can improve your situation through the power of thought, just as surely as you can destroy a positive life with negative thinking. Success begins with an honest analysis of your present condition, acceptance of responsibility for your own life, and the development of a workable plan to achieve what you desire.

—*Think and Grow Rich*

— REFLECTION —

I had to evaluate my mental state honestly, whether or not I liked the result. I was the only person who was responsible for my future.

# CHAPTER 8:

## HITTING ROCK BOTTOM

I would hit absolute rock bottom in 2015.

We think of highs and lows, but this is the year that a seemingly bottomless pit opened up to swallow me.

I was struggling financially and physically, still on prescription drugs and operating at perhaps five percent of my mental capacity. My perceptions were so fogged that I wasn't thinking about my diminished capacity—it had become the new normal. And in this new normal, I had no powerful ideas for my next successful business, no clear strategy for regaining what I had lost, let alone building anything greater.

I still had an established, ingrained habit of trying out whatever came into my mind or into my path. I did try a few humble ventures, all of which promptly failed. Then I came across Xerveo, a company that clearly had some potential for growth. Even in my suboptimal mental state, I managed to raise $1 million for its purchase, and after three months had managed to triple sales. *Finally*, I thought, *I am back on my way.*

### Losing Control.

Seeing the clear success of the business, the major investor in Xerveo desperately sought complete control. At the same time, my psychiatrist (who, by the way, later lost his medical license) kept increasing the dosages of my drugs since I was building up resistance. The cycle continued as the drugs caused me to fall into an even deeper depression and feelings of hopelessness. The pit grew wider and wider.

I had no liquidity—I couldn't immediately pull any money from the company—and I was constantly fighting with the major investor. I was trapped, or so I believed, worse off than when I was sleeping on the streets at 12 or battling the government's attempt to put me away for 100 years.

During that year, I often couldn't sleep at all, and on one night of particular torment, I compensated by taking too many sleeping pills. I ended up in an ambulance, but after being admitted at Cedar Sinai hospital, I flatlined and was officially dead for 20 minutes. A priest had been requested in order to perform last rites.

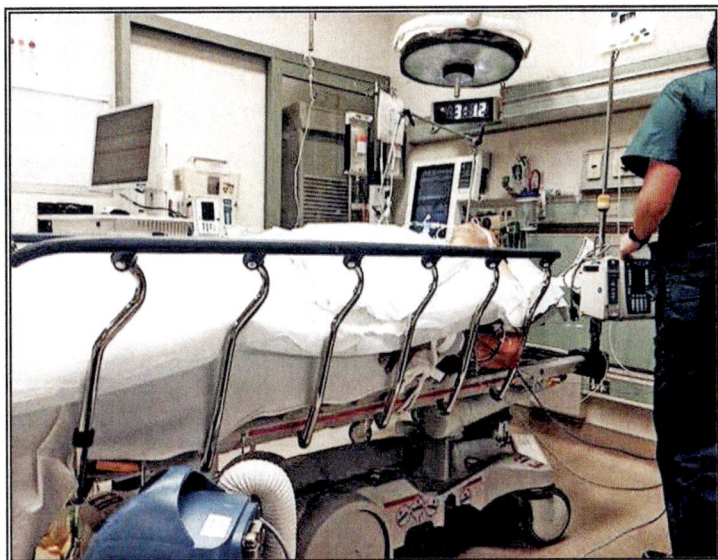

*Death, Life, and Sanity.*

The doctors, fortunately, didn't call an official time of death and instead managed to revive me, after which I spent three weeks in recovery. From Cedar Sinai, I was sent to a mental institution for observation since my overdose was classified as an attempted suicide. This would not be my only time in such a place, either.

At that point, many of my friends and associates didn't think much of my chances for succeeding in life, and I thought that they were correct as long as I remained on psychiatric drugs that blocked my full mental and physical capacities. (But not all: A handful of people never doubted that I could succeed ultimately. Even this miserable experience with all its attendant pain helped clarify the true meaning of trust.)

There was one solution: Go cold turkey, with no long discussions or fallback plan. In my case, that meant a three-month period of withdrawal that, to outside observers, looked very much like those mentally-ill people I encountered on the streets of Tampa so many years before. Like them, I wandered for a while on the streets, homeless and disheveled, sometimes mumbling incoherently or, unfortunately, speaking in a way that made me sound like a danger to myself. I sustained multiple accidental physical injuries.

The authorities apprehended me, after which I was institutionalized for my own protection. This happened twice.

*On the street with $21 to my name.*

Our strength grows out of our weakness, said Ralph Waldo Emerson. "Not until we are pricked and stung and sorely shot at, awakens the indignation which arms itself with secret forces." Strife and struggle can inspire you to overcome adversity and to propel yourself to real achievement. View every struggle as an opportunity for personal growth. It is the struggle itself, not the result that builds character. If you know you are right, stay the course even though the whole world seems to be against you and everyone you know questions your judgment. When you prevail—and you eventually will if you stick to the job—they will all tell you that they knew all along you could do it.

—Think and Grow Rich

At various times in my life, other people told me that I couldn't possibly
succeed. I knew that they were wrong,
which meant that I felt no need to argue about their views. Instead, I just
went ahead and demonstrated how to
apply the principles of *Think and Grow
Rich.*

The light finally started shining through, and the pit disappeared, all
during my last institutionalization, when I finally felt free of the
drugs. I was myself again—in fact, I immediately asked for a pad and
paper so that I could take notes and sketch out a torrent of new business ideas. This wasn't a manic phase, but instead a return to my
previous state, though overlayed with the need to catch up to where
I should be at this point in my life.

All this time, that major investor was angling for a way to completely neutralize my power, and even tried to have me recommitted for a longer period. But I had regained full clarity and convinced the judge in charge of my case that I was completely sane. I had no financial resources at this point, except for my reawakened mind, but that would be enough to rekindle my burning desire for success.

There are a few occasions during our brief time on earth when most of us experience great flashes of insight, great moments of truth that forever change the course of our lives. Most of those experiences result from spectacular failures, not from outstanding successes. It is from the failures that so chagrined and dismayed us that we learn the most lasting lessons. When you are the unwilling recipient of a great moment of truth, extract the useful lessons and then put the entire episode behind you. Learn from your failures, forget about them, and move on to better things.

—*Think and Grow Rich*

## — REFLECTION —

I found that horrific experiences really did pay off. I would find a new level of creative energy that otherwise might have eluded me.

We all have within us the potential for greatness or for failure. Both possibilities are an innate part of our character. Whether we reach for the stars or plunge to the depths of despair depends in large measure on how we manage our positive and negative potential. It is doubtful that, if left unchecked, your virtues will rage out of control. Unfortunately, the reverse is not true about your faults. Left unattended, faults have a way of multiplying until they eventually choke out your good qualities. The surest way to control your faults is to attack them the moment they appear.

*—Think and Grow Rich*

My character is clear to anyone who spends time with me. I don't create openings for bad habits to become established.

# CHAPTER 9:

## THE "IMPOSSIBLE" COMEBACK

I n January, 2016, I was 55 and broke, but now had reoriented on my goal of achieving the great wealth necessary for an extraordinary life.

But many former acquaintances had just melted away, unwilling to consider betting on me. I went to one potential investor after another, focusing especially on those whom I had helped substantially in the past as well as anyone who knew me well, but I was either turned away or ignored. It was impossible, they seemed to think, for me to succeed.

There was one shining exception: my friend John Gray, who had been a part of my life for many years. He always had faith in me and was willing to ride out the ups and downs of the economy, keeping his focus on the long game. He wasn't just someone who wrote about acting with a compassionate spirit—he lived that way too.

Without hesitation, John gave me $10,000 to get back on my feet, no questions asked. I've handled sums many times that amount in my life, but John's contribution remains vivid today. There's a story in *Think and Grow Rich* that centers around a quest to raise $1 million, but that $10,000 was my million: I could take it and create something big.

> *Your clear purpose directs how to use money. Money alone should not direct your purpose.*

### How to Spend Money.

For most people in my situation, that $10,000 would be enough to begin renting a place to live while eventually securing a job that could pay the bills—and that would be about it. But I was in control once again of the principles from *Think and Grow Rich*.

I needed a plan, but, as *Think and Grow Rich* insists, I first needed a "definiteness of purpose," which I could demonstrate by outlining two definite intermediary goals:

- Reacquire the house I lived in before I lost everything.

- Find a business that would jumpstart wealth creation.

I would build from that beginning until I was wealthier than I ever had been.

In order to avoid any poverty mentality, I decided to check into a hotel rather than save money by moving into a cheaper apartment. Within a few months, I had worked out a deal with the owner of my former house so that I could move back in.

*The house in Hollywood Hills that I regained and still live in today.*

Without a plan for your life, it is easier to follow the course of least resistance, to go with the flow, to drift with the current with no particular destination in mind. Having a definite plan for your life greatly simplifies the process of making hundreds of daily decisions that affect your ultimate success. When you know where you want to go, you can quickly decide if your actions are moving you toward your goal or away from it. Without definite, precise goals and a plan for their achievement, each decision must be considered in a vacuum. Definiteness of purpose provides context and allows you to relate specific actions to your overall plan.

—*Think and Grow Rich*

I hold myself and others to the same standard: What is the plan? What is the timeline? And no excuses or alibis.

*The Company That Launched My Comeback.*

I needed to create a high-value company that I then could use as a launching pad for new deals. For the next six months, I tried a few projects that did not pan out, but as usual I was not about to give up.

One day I happened to catch a television report on Carl Icahn pouring $500 million into Lyft, just as the rideshare industry was heating up. I immediately set about developing an original concept that would stand out in the already crowded service space of over a dozen ridesharing apps. Just as Kayak is a metasearch engine for travel sites, my business would search ridesharing apps to find the cheapest ride available.

I had located an essential need that could be met, which is the leverage needed to raise money.

I called the company YayYo, a name that I thought was instantly recognizable and difficult to forget. I pitched the idea to many people, beginning with John, and raised a few million dollars for the launch.

During this time, a new SEC rule was put in place called "Reg A" that allowed taking a company public with more flexibility in raising money, such as soliciting through television advertising, so I created a winning fundraising commercial. Until the SEC changed the rules for Reg A, I was able to raise an additional $5 million.

### New Obstacles and New Battles.

Uber and Lyft, unfortunately, refused to share their APIs (Application Programming Interfaces), which were essential for building the new app. The development money was dwindling fast, and some insiders decided to take advantage of the situation, draining as much money as possible from the company. For a while, YayYo appeared likely to fail.

As *Think and Grow Rich* teaches, rather than just abandon one's goals, figure out a way to shift or pivot, as I have advocated throughout this book. I wasn't going to let down those investors who trusted me and were staying the course. I certainly wouldn't prematurely abandon the company that I deep down knew could take me to the next level of success.

I stepped back, considering the challenges that Uber and Lyft faced. Rather than thinking of them as opponents, I determined what would most benefit *them*: Clearly, both companies had trouble recruiting enough drivers with suitable cars. YayYo would be a company that would buy cars and then rent them to Uber and Lyft drivers who otherwise could not afford to buy them on their own.

The pivot worked spectacularly. The company took off, expanding rapidly.

YayYo was public, but not listed on an exchange. Since the stock was illiquid, and no additional funds could be raised until the company was officially listed, I filed to be listed on the NASDAQ exchange. To my dismay, the person in charge of the listing process was also involved in the delisting process for GenesisIntermedia. There was roadblock after roadblock thrown my way, and the decision appeared to be entirely at his discretion.

After more than two years of going back and forth with the NASDAQ—a process that normally takes a few months at most—I succeeded in securing the listing for the company, but there was a considerable cost. The conditions included resigning as CEO and member of the board of directors, and stepping back from any direct involvement with the company. I finally agreed so that the original investors would profit, their trust in me repaid. I still retained substantial shares in the company.

The bumpy ride continued, however. As happened before, when I couldn't direct day-to-day operations or turn over a company to managers whose work ethic I trusted, infighting took hold. The new CEO constantly was embroiled in various battles. Then, a few months after I managed to obtain the listing, NASDAQ forced the company to delist itself.

Rather than let the company just fail, I stepped back into a lead role in company operations and decisions, working steadily and with few resources for a year. Then COVID hit, and once again I needed to pivot to save the company from the economic shocks that were sinking other businesses throughout the country.

Because I stayed the course, kept a cool head, and reassured investors that we would triumph, the company ultimately flourished and the stock fully recovered. When I exited, I did so with millions in stock. As of this writing, the company has filed for relisting on NASDAQ and is growing exponentially.

Your world will become what you choose to make it. You can reach great heights of success, or you can settle for a miserable life that is devoid of hope. The choice is yours. When you choose a positive course, you set in motion an unstoppable force that will allow you to have a fulfilling career, the love of your family and friends, good physical and mental health, and all of the other true riches of life. To change your world, you must change it from the inside out. You must begin with yourself. When you choose the course that puts your life on a positive track, you will change your life for the better, and you will also positively influence the people with whom you come in contact.

*—Think and Grow Rich*

My own success touches the lives of many people. A burning desire can result in a multitude of different "riches."

None of this success was through some sort of magic or luck. It was first knowing that *I can do this* and then creating a clear vision so that others come to believe that *We can do this.* I don't speak or think in the language of *maybe* or *if,* and those who spend time in my orbit learn the same habit. The first chapter of this book insisted on no alibis, which is a positive, forward-looking philosophy that you should exhibit every day to reach new levels of success.

# Chapter 10:

## Bigger Than I Ever Was

From 2016 until today in 2021, I achieved goals that most people thought I simply could not reach, especially after losing my fortune and my mental stability.

But when I returned to my path, which now was headed toward an extraordinary life, I quickly and decisively built other companies and partnered in new ventures.

### *Resetting the Millions Mindset to Billions.*

My private equity firm, X, LLC, is moving forward to raise billions of dollars to launch more extremely successful companies. Rather than brag about the future, the proof is in what I will actually accomplish.

### Constant Development.

I developed PDQ Pickup that took advantage of weaknesses in de-livery logistics. The company has grown exponentially during the COVID crisis and currently is worth hundreds of millions of dollars.

EV Mobility, a company that is deploying electric vehicles in apart-ment buildings and hotels as amenities for residents and guests, is anticipated to build a fleet of over 20,000 cars in the next two years and is esti-mated to soon be worth more than $2 billion.

### The Expansion of Media Projects.

Through Extraordinary Life Entertainment, I created and produced the Las Vegas show *27*, which showcases the great musicians who died at 27, such as Robert Johnson, Janis Joplin, Jimmy Hendrix, Jim Morison, Kurt Cobain, and Amy Winehouse. And against the odds, I obtained a residency at the new Virgin Hotel, where *27* quickly has become the most popular show in Las Vegas. I plan through Extraordinary Life Entertainment to produce several more shows and establish a record label to develop new artists.

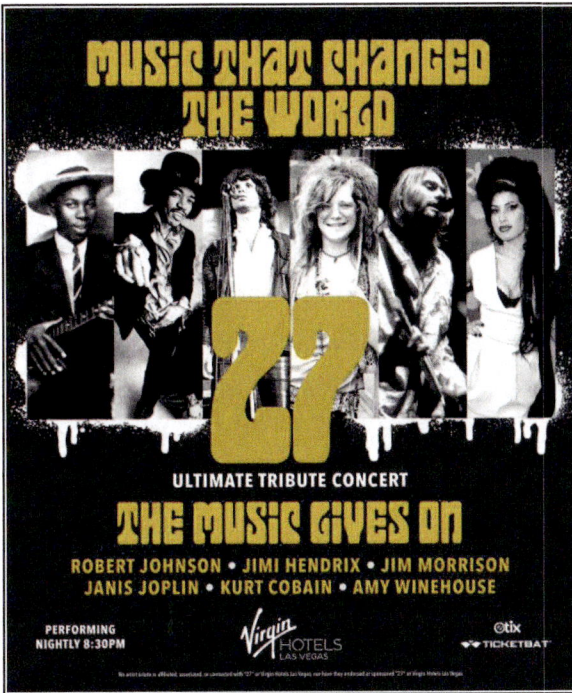

*The cast of 27 on their way to a San Francisco show.*

It is all a matter of attitude. As you grow and develop, make sure your experience is directed toward the acquisition of wisdom, not the acceptance of cynicism. If you find it difficult to keep an open mind because of previous experiences, remind yourself that you're dealing with different people, that conditions have changed, or that because you are older and wiser, your chances of success are greater than in the past.

*—Think and Grow Rich*

I approach people with an honest attitude of learning. To bring them into a new vision requires that I first know what theirs is.

## A Plane Never Is Just a Plane.

I learned early on from Adnan Khashoggi that a plane is one of the most powerful business tools that an entrepreneur can own. My current wide-body jet—with a bedroom, shower, and seating for 19 people—is superior to my previous one and, because of its 10 extra fuel tanks, can be deployed to any location in the world.

Besides acquiring a new, better jet and moving back into my former house in the Hollywood Hills, I located my original 1987 De Tomaso, which I had restored to its former glory.

*My 1987 De Tomaso.*

Since Adnan Khashoggi's death in 2017, no one has been able to step in as a powerbroker whom world leaders can trust. Certainly, there are now objectively richer people, but he deployed his wealth to negotiate mega-deals between large corporations and heads of state. In my years with him, I learned the strategies essential for this level of success, and remain one of the few people in the world who knows how to create and even surpass his accomplishments while striving for a truly extraordinary life.

One of my main goals moving forward is to fill the void that Adnan left behind by becoming a powerbroker on his level. I have no doubt that I will accomplish this and much, much more.

---

One of the most common mistakes is making excuses to explain why we do not succeed. Unfortunately, the vast majority of people in the world—those who do not succeed—are excuse-makers. They try to explain their action, or inaction, with words. When you succeed, accept the congratulations of others with good grace; when you fail, take responsibility for your actions, learn from your mistakes, and move on to more constructive things. When your actions are appropriate in every circumstance, you will never feel the need to explain them with words. Your actions will say all that needs to be said.

—*Think and Grow Rich*

---

If I focus on all the *Think and Grow Rich* principles for success, I never will be tempted to resort to an alibi.

$$\wedge\!\!\!\sqrt{}$$

### No Alibis.

I had to start over many times in life. I have not used any excuses or alibis that often block progress on the path to success. I overcame lack of education and money; intense criticism; a fight with the government; prescription drugs; and even death.

Starting over with absolutely nothing, I was able to rebuild wealth to the hundreds of millions and soon to be in the billions. I was able to succeed in the face of adversity without making excuses for failure.

If you believe in yourself and follow the principles laid out in *Think and Grow Rich* as well as the keys that I have found during my life, there is nothing to stop you from achieving an extraordinary life of success too.

# CHAPTER 11:

## MY STANDARD OPERATING PROCEDURE

I wrote this book to inspire you, rather than relive my old glories and accomplishments, let alone wallow in the worst times.

As I've repeatedly insisted, I've always focused on moving forward, and I want you to do the same.

I've tied my business and personal philosophy to what I inherited from *Think and Grow Rich*, demonstrating to myself and others that its principles can be adapted to whatever life throws our way. Eventually, I realized that a merely "successful" life wasn't enough and that "extraordinary" was a word more closely aligned with my ultimate goal.

### Expectations and Deals.

Along my journey, I did manage to create many extraordinary experiences for myself and my friends and associates. I've been one of those legendary high-rollers in Las Vegas, though gambling was entertainment for me, not to mention a way to connect to other potential business investors for whom the high life is just their everyday world.

When you reset your expectations of what a "standard" deal is, you move from thousands to millions and eventually on to billions. And sometimes the gambling life does provide an important strategy: If you are unwilling to ever go all in, 100% if necessary, it is unlikely that you can become one of the main players on the world stage, which, first inspired by Adnan Khashoggi's example, is what I intend to be.

I actually don't spend *any* time worrying about what other people think of me. I actually do care, however, about inspiring people, so take what you can from my journey and use it to propel yourself onward.

### Possessions.

Particular acquisitions don't have a strong hold on my mind. They are potential tools that can help me build an international reputation that in turn can be leveraged in order to structure immense deals, just as Adnan Khashoggi used his acquisitions to become a head of state without a state.

Though I do have possessions that give me pleasure, I do not let them control me. I determined the minimum that I need to live comfortably, and as I demonstrated when sold my possessions to follow Adnan, anything else can be regained (or not) as needed.

In short, I've learned to avoid too much sentimentality about what I materially own, though I have made it a point of pride to reacquire touchstones—such as a jet—of my journey to the extraordinary life.

### How My Mind Works.

Losing any of my mental capacity led to the lowest point of my life. I'll describe what my mind, when it is functioning in what I consider a normal mode, is like.

Imagine not just a file cabinet, but a boundless room with a virtually unlimited supply of drawers. I am able to access any file at any time, no matter what is going on around me. I don't have a short attention span, either. Instead, I can give each file my undivided attention for as long as is needed and strictly compartmentalize any topics or issues.

The same applies to my daily schedule, which includes many, many interactions with people. Whatever the circumstances, I give each person my complete, focused attention during that time, however brief or long, then move on to another call, text, email, or meeting.

My personal life always has worked just the same: If I am with a friend or romantic partner, I am completely focused on that person.

(This is one reason why I stayed on good terms with my exes. I always was completely "on" during the time we had.)

I usually am awake no later than 5 am and go to bed around midnight, and if I have a new idea or insight, I might get up at 4 am. I'll have a cup of coffee when I wake up, but other than that, I use no chemical aids, and I don't drink.

I do research before the market opens, monitor and complete stock trades throughout the day, speak with easily more than a dozen people over the phone, and visit various offices and businesses—and that is just a sample. I am as likely to speak with a mechanic who services a company's Tesla as I am to speak to a CEO. I'm always on the lookout for new opportunities.

When you train your mind to seek out opportunities, you will find that every day literally presents you with more opportunities than you can take advantage of. They will be all around you. Instead of your seeking opportunities, they will seek you out. Your biggest problem will be choosing the best ones. The first step in making sure you are ready to recognize opportunities when they occur is to make sure you have a clear understanding of your own core competencies. Realistically assess your strengths and weaknesses as though you were reviewing the credentials of a total stranger. Identify what areas you're best in and those where you need improvement. Work on your weaknesses and build upon your strengths so that when you recognize opportunities you are prepared to capitalize upon them.

—*Think and Grow Rich*

I constantly inventory my assets: What do I have now that can be leveraged advantageously? Again and again, the most essential assets are my mental abilities.

I hear *No* all the time. As I remarked earlier in the book, I always proceed as though there is a yes behind that no. When I learned that my new jet, which I had extensively remodeled, would not be ready to fly for two weeks, I sat on board with my consultants, asked questions, and then listened quietly, allowing silences to open up. Then I would ask more questions and wait. I never raised my voice or became visibly angry.

The plane needed to fly in the next two days so that I and my associates could fly to Las Vegas to see the musical show I had produced and promoted. Eventually, I was assured that the updates would be completed on time. The no became a yes.

Though I move quickly and decisively from one person or issue to another, I am not jumpy or nervous. I admire the trait of gracefulness when it means moving at a smooth, controlled rhythm. It's just that my rhythm seems to be faster than the average person's.

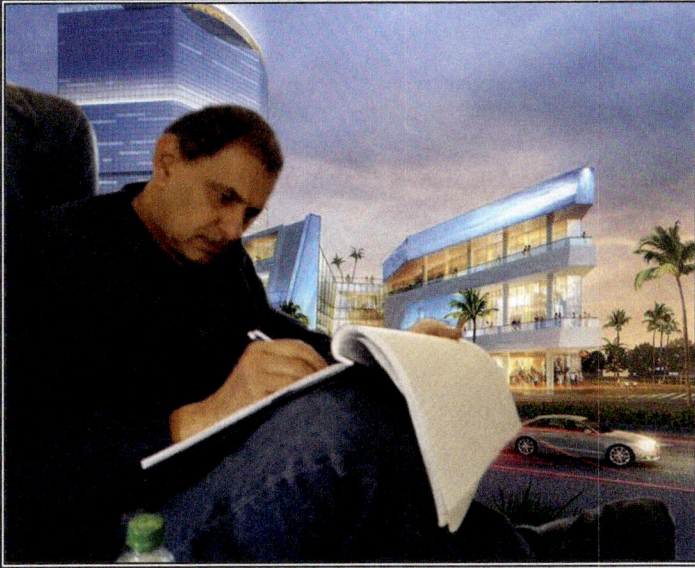

*Always creating and strategizing.*

I prize my ability to think a few steps ahead of others, just as chess experts have to consider the possible moves of their opponents. My way of thinking and acting was—and is—completely natural. Like a goldfish swimming through water in an aquarium, I hardly noticed the water until it was taken away, leaving me gasping for breath.

There are many things in life that you cannot control, but you can always control your attitude toward them. Defeat is never permanent unless you allow it to be so. When you have a positive attitude, you will recognize failure for the impostor that it is and realize that it is really a learning experience, a valuable lesson that will help you succeed with the next attempt. Ask yourself: What could I have done differently that would have altered the outcome? What can I do in the future to minimize problems and mistakes? What did I learn from this experience that I can put to good use next time? If you approach obstacles and setbacks with a positive attitude, you will be surprised how quickly you can turn defeat into victory.

—*Think and Grow Rich*

I cannot control the role of the dice in
a casino, but I can control how I face
wins and losses, especially by using
the latter to inform my future actions.

## What's the End Game?

At some point, extremely rich people do face the question of what
comes next. In my case, I'm still working on a life that propels me to
a wider stage, one that not only is international in scope, but that
offers even more creative possibilities. I'm going to continue to
build companies, services, products, and, most of all, powerful ideas
that can change the world.

In a previous chapter, I mentioned my appearance on the charity
circuit, but only briefly since to discuss that at length would seem to
be just bragging or preening. But one issue that I have been associ-
ated with previously is defeating homelessness, especially given my
direct experience. I'm thinking about how eventually I can make an
impact on this social issue, so stay tuned to see what happens.

YOU ARE INVITED TO ATTEND THE
ANNUAL HUMANITARIAN OF THE YEAR AWARD
GIVEN BY
DONALD T. STERLING HOMELESS & MEDICAL CENTER
HONORING

RAMY EL-BATRAWI
HUMANITARIAN OF THE YEAR
FOR HIS SUPPORT OF THE HOMELESS PEOPLE OF LOS ANGELES

MONDAY, JUNE 26, 2006

SPAGO
176 NORTH CANON DRIVE  BEVERLY HILLS
COCKTAILS AT 6:30PM      DINNER AT 7:30PM

SPECIAL GUESTS WILL INCLUDE
NATALIE COLE, LEE IACCOCA, BERRY GORDY, JR.,
AUTHOR JOHN GRAY, BISHOP CHARLES BLAKE, DON CORNELIUS,
DON JOHNSON, SMOKEY ROBINSON, DICK VAN DYKE,
MARCUS ALLEN, JIM BROWN, WILLIE GAULT, PEDRO FERRE
AND MANY MORE SUPPORTERS OF THE HOMELESS

PRODUCED BY TAMI BENNETT    DIRECTED BY DIANA MILLER

RSVP TO DIANA MILLER 310.573.9649

BY INVITATION ONLY      (NON-TRANSFERABLE)

*I have been homeless more than once, and I have been part of efforts to address homelessness for many years.*

I want to end this chapter by reminding you that the principles of *Think and Grow Rich* can be applied to every aspect of your life, and not just the attainment of wealth, so that you can achieve whatever goal you set for yourself, such as winning great love.

Eighteen months before publishing this book, I met the woman of my dreams, Courtney Corso. She declined to go on a date with me for four months, but no matter how many times I heard *no*, I pursued her with the same focus and burning desire that I apply to any important, worthwhile goal. A year and a half later, she accepted my proposal, and now we are married.

# CONCLUSION:

# HOW WILL YOU ANSWER THE QUESTION?

After reading this book, you know that for decades I've answered the question, *Can you think and growth rich?* with a resounding *Yes!*

You now need to answer that question for yourself. The stories of others' success have inspired me, and I hope that you take away something from this book that will inspire you as well.

Every one of my losses was an opportunity to demonstrate that the "ghosts of fear" had no power over me, that it was possible to move forward without alibis, without the *What Ifs* that too many people are tempted to offer. My experience can help reassure you when others doubt you, which they surely will at some point, or when you begin to doubt yourself. You must push past doubt if you are devoted to achieving tremendous financial rewards and the lifestyle that accompanies them.

We all can carve out our own unique paths. Mine, I have realized, is aimed at what I call an extraordinary life that is as elevated above my first "rich" life in Tampa as that was above my homeless street life when I first arrived in the city. I still credit *Think and Grow Rich* with the scaffolding I used to build the person I am, but in the spirit of that book and Napoleon Hill's other work, here are my keys that can unlock many doors to success. If you can improve on them, all the better.

## 28 Keys to the Extraordinary Life.

Mix what you want with intense emotions in order to drive you to ever greater success.

Determination and a burning desire can never be stopped.

Discard doubt, but do not discard those who have helped you and believed in you.

When you find words that inspire you to a greater future, keep them in the front of your mind at all times.

Make your hope of gain greater than your fear of loss.

Find the need and fill it.

To achieve an extraordinary life, step with, and not on or over, people who believe in you.

To build bigger and faster, use other people's money.

When using other people's money, you have to take responsibility, and you have to put them ahead of you.

At all times, have faith in yourself and what you can accomplish.

Always be ready to shift when you're headed in the wrong direction.

Always show confidence when you speak. Others are drawn to those who speak and act confidently.

Success requires taking risks when you have to.

A good deal = everyone wins.

More is lost through indecision than the wrong decision.

Trust is gained by working in others' best interests.

Work with others, not for others.

Constantly inventory your true assets, even if it is just a single burning desire.

We all have at least one great idea, but it is useless without decisive action.

Find the yes behind the no.

Focus on what you and others can build.

Conversations always are opportunities to learn about and align visions.

Educate yourself about the challenges you encounter.

Adversity is never permanent.

If you can control your own mind, you will never be controlled by the mind of another.

Victory is always possible for the person who refuses to stop fighting.

All failures are temporary.

Your clear purpose directs how to use money. Money alone should not direct your purpose.

I learned to make physical keys in my business venture for the Zayre department store chain all those years ago. Since then, I keep moving forward, confident that every door in my way can be unlocked, every obstacle or challenge turned into an opportunity, every no turned into a yes.

Use Napoleon Hill's principles to unlock your potential. Begin with a burning desire that is ignited by powerful emotions, whether positive or negative.

Where you go next is entirely up to you.

# A LAST WORD FROM THE AUTHOR

M y journey is proof that the principles of *Think and Grow Rich* really do work. I wasn't born with any special or unusual powers. The way I think was built over time with focused effort. You can do the same if you link your decision with concrete action while making your hope of gain greater than your fear of loss.

I plan to make the next years the most productive of my life.

Printed in Great Britain
by Amazon

29033723R00099